# DIVINE PURPOSE
*Rising in Feminine Power*

Rachel White

**BALBOA.**
PRESS
A DIVISION OF HAY HOUSE

Copyright © 2019 Rachel White.

All rights reserved. No part of this book may be used or reproduced by any means, graphic, electronic, or mechanical, including photocopying, recording, taping or by any information storage retrieval system without the written permission of the author except in the case of brief quotations embodied in critical articles and reviews.

New Revised Standard Version Bible, copyright © 1989 the Division of Christian Education of the National Council of the Churches of Christ in the United States of America. Used by permission. All rights reserved.

Balboa Press books may be ordered through booksellers or by contacting:

Balboa Press
A Division of Hay House
1663 Liberty Drive
Bloomington, IN 47403
www.balboapress.co.uk
1 (877) 407-4847

Because of the dynamic nature of the Internet, any web addresses or links contained in this book may have changed since publication and may no longer be valid. The views expressed in this work are solely those of the author and do not necessarily reflect the views of the publisher, and the publisher hereby disclaims any responsibility for them.

The author of this book does not dispense medical advice or prescribe the use of any technique as a form of treatment for physical, emotional, or medical problems without the advice of a physician, either directly or indirectly. The intent of the author is only to offer information of a general nature to help you in your quest for emotional and spiritual well-being. In the event you use any of the information in this book for yourself, which is your constitutional right, the author and the publisher assume no responsibility for your actions.

Any people depicted in stock imagery provided by Getty Images are models, and such images are being used for illustrative purposes only.
Certain stock imagery © Getty Images.

Print information available on the last page.

ISBN: 978-1-9822-8070-3 (sc)
ISBN: 978-1-9822-8071-0 (e)

Balboa Press rev. date: 05/30/2019

# TABLE OF CONTENTS

Introduction .................................................................ix
1   The Universe ................................................. 1
2   Heart Connection ......................................11
3   Three Feminine Superpowers....................19
4   Our Ancient Ancestor Sisters .....................37
5   Empowerment..............................................43
6   Divine Purpose............................................ 54
7   Your Divine Purpose ...................................58
8   The Wounded Feminine..............................72
9   The Inner She and the Outer She ..............79
10  Sit on Your Throne, and Wear Your Crown............. 94
11  A Gathered Sisterhood ..............................105
12  Rising and Flowing ...................................111
13  Legacy of a Heart Maiden.........................116

Dedicated to every woman of the world who owns a beautiful heart. Especially my own sweet Suzanna Emillie

# INTRODUCTION

Hey, sister, I want you to know that this book has come from a special place. I've been developing my divine purpose for a while now. As I lean in and listen to the universe as a life force calling deep into my heart, I hear something so very special, golden. We are on a journey together. I feel the call so deeply. My hope is that our beautiful, feminine hearts all over the world gather together in an amazing sacred connection to understand who we fully are in the universe that brought us into being.

I have a knowing that the universe called me to be an empowerer as my divine purpose. Being faithful to that call led me to share my heart with you about how you can find your own divine purpose—how each of us can begin to get our hearts aligned with love and light and life. I long to see me, you, all of us resolved in our feminine, understanding and dealing with so many of the things that have come into our lives to keep us small, damped down, crushed, and defeated.

It is surely time to change how our hearts understand the message about what it means to be inside our true feminine. Join me, sister, in this journey. Together we are going to be able to weave and flow together. These pages contain my heart. I know you will catch the essence of what I'm sharing. We are going to explore lots of things very deeply.

On the way, I want you to know you are supported. Please join us at divinepurpose.co.uk and the *Divine Purpose—Rising in feminine power* Facebook group. Our sisters there are waiting to love and hold you. You are so welcome. Come join us!

Something life affirming, new, is waiting to be birthed. A change is going to come, and it's coming to our hearts first. I want to bring us a challenge straight into the pain of the wounded feminine that we've so normalised—the recognition that there is a reckoning, an awakening, an arising of the feminine. That we have superpowers and that we walk as queens. A reclaiming of what could and should be. It's time. Can you hear the deep call of the earth, the moon, the sisterhood? For our daughters, our young maidens, a new day, a new sunrise is coming.

I'm hopeful that in these pages, there'll be new discoveries, the aha light bulb moments. May our hearts be revealed, resolved, healed. There is new clarity to be found here. I'm holding space for you as you read. Take your time to just be with yourself as the universe shows you your truth.

Are you ready, girlfriend? Ready to face this feeling that you've had for so long but can't quite put your finger on? Ready to find out why the universe has placed you here? To know your divine purpose. To be fulfilled within it. To finally come home to yourself. To align with a universe so full of power you'll feel like you've caught fire. As you read this book, my intention is to light your touch paper for great things. I already know that the universe holds you for you are precious, and we need you, sister, to stand with us. For this is truly your time to rise. To become a world changer through your divine purpose.

With much love,
Rachel xxx

# CHAPTER 1

# *The Universe*

> The secrets of the Universe are found in energy, frequency, and vibration.
> —Nikola Tesla (1856–1943)

My darling sister, how much do we know about the universe that sent us, that breathed us into life with a future, a past, and a destiny? Do we know anything? How could we know that the universe holds all creation within itself, yet resides within us at the same time?

The mystery of it is completely profound, misunderstood, and cannot be completely known. It is that deep knowing of something bigger and greater than ourselves—the life force—that solidifies in us the strength of who we are.

The universe we often think about is presented to us in a scientific context. It contains our earth, distant galaxies, planets, moon, and, of course, the sun. That universe immediately becomes the image in our minds if we mention it. However, whilst true, there is a lot more complexity to it than just that.

Everything vibrates. Yes, every object inside the universe, including you and I, resonates at its own frequency. Some perceive this as energy which means that everything has its own place of resonance. The universe is ordered but not as we understand "order" in schemes of hierarchy and ranking, but by love, light, and life. This is the vibration of the whole universe. How amazing to be enveloped into a universe that has at its very core, and indeed its extremities, pure love.

That's good news for us, sisters. Do you see what this means? The universe all around us sends out positive vibes of love through everything. How could it be anything else? You see, as a creative force, the universe has breathed life through pure love into everything it created, everything it touched. This means, my darling, regardless of your conception, birth, and every experience you ever have. Ultimately, you and I, as feminine beings, were created from pure love. The purest love, to embody love, from a source (some say God) that cannot help but love us deeply. Creation itself, the natural world, is an act of and an expression of love. Effects of it are around us all the time. How amazing is that?

The call of our hearts is to respond as loved and held beings. This is our longing; it is embedded deep within. Our modern culture and lifestyle tend to dumb this down, attempting to numb it out of us by making demands on our spiritual selves through a mixed-up bombardment of human-made distractions. So deep down, it may remain hidden, buried, squashed until an amazing moment of awakening, that often comes from crisis or event we didn't choose, occurs. Our new realisation is that there is more to us, more to our lives than our current experiences, our distresses, our nine-to-five constructs of a world, imported beliefs, and even

*Divine Purpose*

the name given to us at birth. The understanding of self-identity within a framework of expectations indicates we are infinite as spiritual beings, able to access all that the universe holds for us. Which, when we think it through, must be nothing less than creative, life force power. Some would say that we are not merely human beings having spiritual experiences but spiritual beings having human ones. That's an interesting perspective I tend to agree with.

Many of us have come to the place we are today by travelling a unique journey. None of us have had the exact same experiences which have shaped and moulded us into the people we are. We stand today as products of all that has gone before. There is no blame or judgement; it is what it is. In many cases, it is a sea of heartbreaks mingled with some joys along the way.

Fair to say if you are anything like me, life has happened around you, to you. Oftentimes, we are bystanders in our lives, watching the unfolding of our lives which overwhelms us. Sometimes with a feeling of fast-paced out-of-control-ness. Very occasionally, we've had the chance to pursue and choose our top choices for ourselves. Even when we have, there are those, "If only" I could have/do/be times. Sometimes we got lucky; it worked out how we planned. Then that which we thought would do it for us just didn't. We were left unfulfilled by the thing we wanted, craved, and received, but it was not as we thought it would be. Other times, things happened to us against our consent, our will, making our very souls align with victimhood. We asked then, understandably, where was the universe of pure love, this God, in the most painful, difficult moments?

The truth is, all that matters is this moment, the "right now". The universe doesn't operate as we do, within the definitive of time and space. It is eternal. Everything that has happened to us for better or worse (for some, the worse is really very much worse) has produced the beautiful person we are as we stand today. Some of us, I know, don't feel beautiful as the pain, abuses, and trauma have been great, leaving our hearts tarnished and worn out. We look at ourselves and see the ugliness of all the bad stuff and consider that we are ugly because of it. But this is not the truth, even if we feel that it is. It cannot be true because we were birthed in a spiritual sense by a universe of pure love that cannot create anything outside of pure love. That is who we truly are when all the "stuff" is stripped away it is the fullest truth.

All our experiences contribute to the heart of us as feminine female beings. The truth is, what is next in store for us as provided by the universe wouldn't be accessible to us without these building blocks. In the universe, the platform of suffering has a purpose. No experience is ever wasted. Never.

Of course, that's not saying we like suffering and pain and abuse. No way. We must, of course, stand with each other in those moments. Who would choose those things? No one. It's right to be anti-oppression in all its ugly forms. But reality instructs us that these moments happen. The wonderful thing is that on this journey, when we begin to look at this from the perspective of the awakening of the heart, we can change our understanding. We realise the universe has power enough to help us reconcile and redeem (cancel out) these things. No longer are they just awful happenings, filling us with fear, hate, and bitterness. Instead they are gifts to help our understanding from the inside out. To help us truly understand and know intimately what pure love is. Compassion, tolerance, peace, and many other elements of it can be known. Further along on this journey,

## Divine Purpose

we begin to see how the very thing that birthed pain into our hearts was the defining moment that helped us get clear on our boundaries, our self-identifies, our passions. In other words, the universe helped us learn. It helped us turn around that awful happening. We reap the benefit of the thing intended for our detriment; ultimately, it now contributes towards our good. The universe always wins, *always*. There is no other choice. The universe, being a source of pure love, cannot create in the same space as fear and hate. It's just not possible. It is one or the other.

The remarkable work for us begins as we line up our intentions with a universe of pure love. You see, we can abound in a place of fear and other negative emotions. Each of us is free to do that if we so choose. We have the freedom of choice. But in making that choice, we have to know if our hearts are not aligned with this pure love force. If we are intentional in our resistance, it is likely that we attract even more circumstances into our lives that produce more fear, hate, and bitterness. It is a sad circle, a chain loop of reaction.

I'm hopeful that you can see what I can as I write these words. We, you and I, are in charge of our own realities. There is no handover of responsibility. The universe is not a genie in a bottle, waiting to be rubbed the right way in order to deliver what we want. Or a sulking, brooding cloud ready to hail upon us some kind of destruction. No. It's not like that at all! Our beautiful universe, our life force—some say God—is pure love. Our hearts may align with its vibe, not the other way around. So in this free-will choice, what will we choose?

How we line up with the universe of pure love determines our choices. We fit into its plans for us with confidence, knowledge, and trust. Our understanding is the universe that sent us breathed us into being through pure love and will hold us, and give us the ability to walk in a place of fulfilment because we commit to what the universe has designed for us, our unique divine purpose. We, each one of us, have been chosen for such a time as this. When we begin to tap into this, we begin to understand that this is the birth seat of our very own divine purpose.

Okay, sister, let's just breathe a minute. Those who know me know I'm big on journaling. I find it so helpful. So if you haven't already, get a sparkly notebook and a pencil. Write down anything that comes up for you as we journey together through these thoughts. I promise it will be worth it. Take some time to unpack your thoughts about the universe, the awesomeness of it. Meditate on how much love and acceptance you can feel as you connect. Breathe it in.

The universe emanates energy in two forms, masculine and feminine. We know this absolutely to be true. It is represented not only in human beings but in the animal kingdom. Even plants have male and female parts. Furthermore, night and day are equally representative, as is the sun and moon, of this duality. The masculine and feminine are different, but they are also complementary. Within the universe, this duality flows in and out and around itself. Neither is stronger nor weaker than the other; they are balanced. Together they make the whole. For the very continuation of the human race, both the male and female essence is needed. Creation cannot continue without full participation of both the masculine and the feminine.

So what does this mean for us born into a female body? For sure we need to explore what true femininity is. How we can express it and magnify it. In some cases, reclaim it and own it so that our femininity may serve us. In later chapters, we explore what this feminine identity is all about. We know that both the masculine and feminine elements

## Divine Purpose

of how we are as humans have been hijacked and corrupted over centuries. The reason for this, in part, is because females have been stripped of their wild feminine power as given to them by the universe and offered substitutes along the way through human-made constructs of how a woman should be. It has been handed down to us through fear, patriarchy, expectations, ideologies, and religious fervour. I'm interested in who the universe says I am. Aren't you? The source that sent us, birthed us, and gave us our divine purposes to emanate through our female bodies. The universe that sent us and breathed us into being is strong enough to hold us and show us the way. It is into that energy that we tap. Let it open like a floodgate, so we may know who we truly are.

Bring it on, sister. But more than that, let it be birthed in our hearts. Our beautiful, feminine hearts are just longing to connect with the universe in profound ways. To become open and soft and malleable to that which the universe would have us learn. The heartbeat of the universe is expressed—"expressed" is too small a word; "teeming over without containment and exploding" is more like it—through creation, nature. This is where the idea of the term "Mother Earth" originates, and it is very appropriate. The earth is indeed like a mother to us, bringing comfort, restoration, healing, and sustenance. Our religious ideology often funnels us to consider God as solely male, but this cannot be the truth. God is our life force and is equally female and male. The beauty and wonder of all this life force has created are wildly presented before us all the time. If we have no spiritual history of connecting with the universe, this is a great place to start. Getting immersed in the natural world and swimming with its flow often kick-starts our hearts back to life.

## Rachel White

Try as an exercise for a week or so, until it becomes habit, to walk inside nature. This can be done without coming out of our daily routines. It's about awakening, reviving that dormant sense of us that has been damped down. Throughout your day, pluck a flower, touch the bark of a tree, really hold a leaf or a stone. Notice everything about how it feels, how it smells. Begin to connect with it, give thanks for it, identify how it relates to how you feel in that moment. Is it strong? Is it fragile? Take time to notice how the trees move in the wind, how cold or hot the temperature is. The direction of the rain. The shape of clouds. How water feels on your skin. How herbs and spices in your kitchen really smell and taste. How a candle flame flickers. How water boils in a pan. You get the idea. The possibilities are endless.

This is how we begin to create flow—a spiritual conversation, a connection with the universe. Allow nature to speak to your heart and your spirit. You'll be amazed at what happens when we begin this. Our energy changes, and people around us begin to pick up on it. They may not identify what it is, but they will notice. And we will begin to know ourselves better within this beautiful universe.

The feminine is all about flow and curves, weaving, intertwining, creating. The masculine is all about straight lines, logic, black and white. Yes or no questions and answers. So in becoming more feminine, we need to access this flow and enhance it in every way. Introduce real plants and flowers into our living spaces and soft fabrics into our furnishings and clothing. Lean towards the curvy edges, the quirky, the colourful, and away from the straight edge, sharp corners, or spikes. Music could be soft or flowing or ambient nature sounds as background filler, rather than constant TV when we are not really watching it or jangly,

## Divine Purpose

harsh music. To fill our living environments that promote and reflect curves, weaves, asymmetry and the natural world is so helpful. These simple adjustments speak into our hearts on a deep level and enhance the flow of the feminine.

The flow of the feminine needs to be switched on in our hearts. I guarantee that when we intentionally pursue the universe with this, the universe will respond in a very beautiful, sacred way. That's how it works. Something profound will happen, I guarantee. You will notice and recognise it for what it is. Boom! Please do share your experiences with this on our Facebook pages as it encourages us all. It's exciting.

The most sacred of all flowing, weaving, and connecting with the universe is the ability to co-create. The ultimate purpose of the universe is to expand. So in being a creator, or accessing our creative sides, instantly connects us to the universe. Whether we grow a baby or a plant, paint a picture, or move our bodies in the privacy of our own front rooms, Go create something, anything. That's what I'm doing with this book. It is a creation. I'm creating with the universe, bringing a gift to your heart and fulfilling my divine purpose as an empowerer all at the same time. See how it works? Awesomeness!

The feminine is all about flow and curves and weaving. The entirety of this book is relevant to understanding divine purpose. I've deliberately saved the intimate details for later chapters before diving right in. My heart feels that in order to get to that place, we first need to go on a journey of exploration and understanding. Our hearts need to be connected to the universe and with each other as a sacred grounding which we will work through in these early chapters.

So, my darling, take some time now to ponder, process,

and journal your thoughts. Spend some time in nature. Connect with the universe that sent you. Take some time for you before we move to our next chapter.

# CHAPTER 2

# *Heart Connection*

I am the captain of my own soul.
—Nelson Mandela (1918–2013)

To be heart connected is incredible. It is the very synchronisation of two living hearts beating at the same pace, in unison. Two hearts that are not the same but are joined by unseen bonds. A physical metaphor, really, for what occurs at a spiritual level, and a theme we've all heard a million times over in popular love songs. But is it really that simplistic, that obvious to grasp? Well, yes and no. The heart connection we explore here is far deeper than the concept of it gleaned through a love song to the masses. I'm hoping you'll understand while reading through the chapter on the universe that this goes deep—deeper than we've realised. Our universe that has breathed its life into our souls and sent us on a love mission to the world has done so in trust that we would choose its way, the way of love. We are not cast adrift like a lonely voyager, one girl in a boat on her own in the middle of a desolate sea. Although, it can often feel this way. The truth is that this is not the case. Not at all. Or at least it shouldn't be.

Our hearts remain deeply connected, embedded into the universe. The way in which it works is that the universe releases us into free will. It cannot dictate to us who or what we should be, or what we should do with the gifts it equipped us with. Or how to treat others. We are completely free of its control. That is ultimate freedom, and it absolutely has to be this way. Anything less is, of course, not pure love. Pure love cannot control; it simply asks for a response. This is the position we find ourselves in as spiritual beings. It goes some way in explaining why the universe does not intervene in a crisis to allow no suffering borne from one person to another. The perpetrator, if there is one, of our suffering is under the same free will to respond to the universe in his or her dealings with others on a love basis, the same as you and I.

So that's the cry of our hearts, that we be fully connected, plugged into this power source of infinite love. All of us feel it, even if we are in denial. It is why, in our own spiritual DNA, we long to be really understood and loved. We know that place we go to inside, where we feel the joy and the pain. That feeling or sensation, the emotional and spiritual resonance is the cry of our heart longing for this deep connection.

We've largely misunderstood that the universe is waiting for a response from us, from our hearts. That we ourselves would lead the way into heart connection. The universe has handed us the power to be in charge of this relationship. It is our hearts that must respond to its calling.

What has happened to separate us from this beautiful

## Divine Purpose

source of pure love? Many things that come in the form of distractions from the source come through our physical and emotional senses. In some ways, we are in survival mode as human beings and have been for millions of years, concentrating and prioritising our physical needs above all else. This has been highly necessary certainly; the continuation of humans is at stake if not. But there is a deeper understanding, one that has been hidden, damped down, ignored, and ridiculed. In the case of women, squashed, threatened, and often forced out of us.

You see, to be heart connected to the universe means that we are fully able to access its power. Its ultimate foundation is that of love and wholeness and goodness. So the power that comes from it is also rooted in those things. The power to heal, the power to restore, the power to create, the power to empower, all these things and more are there waiting for us to realise our place in claiming them. Being heart connected into this place means that as humans, we can express the very heart of the universe for the complete benefit of all who inhabit planet Earth.

The question is then, how do we get heart connected in—or back in, we could say? For sure, we have to open up our hearts to hear what the universe is saying specifically to us. Here's the thing though. This wonderful universe—our source, founded on love and life—is only going to input into our lives on that basis. Only when we ourselves seek it will it respond. This is where the first premise of loving ourselves originates. It is the universe that gives us the power to love ourselves. When we have been unloved, it has the power to give us self-esteem, confidence, and inner strength. Our divine purpose comes straight out of seeking a response from the life source. Its response to us in that moment is founded on our deep awakening, knowing that we are loved and held right within its power. We begin communicating with this energy in ways we hadn't previously understood.

The universe is powerless if we make it so. To turn our backs and harden our hearts makes our source of love invisible to us. The universe will never push us in any direction. It is simply there waiting for us to respond. My darling, did you just realise what we said there? You and I have the power to direct the universe itself into action on our behalf. Did you catch that? Read that again. Boom!

Because the universe is pure love, that is the exchange between our heart and its heart. That's where our deep knowing comes from.

Now, as we begin our first glimpse of what heart connectedness is all about, our desire for it explodes tenfold.

Here are some ways to boost our heart connectedness with the universe.

- Open our hearts and become soft in our approaches to everything that is a life form. Connect with the natural world as we explored in chapter 1.
- Take nothing personally; look at each interaction for what it is, and intentionally choose not to react as though the incoming is a personal attack which needs to be defended.
- Receive; be open to receive well. Welcome others for their help, offers of positivity, and compliments.
- Be welcoming and invitational with others. Hold others in a safe place by engaging them through good eye contact and smiles.

These simple measures run deep. As we realise that other people are also vessels of the universe in the same way that we are, our understanding strengthens.

## Divine Purpose

Our heart connections with other people can be profound. As women on a heart journey, it naturally follows that we will pursue heart connections with many people in our lives. My darling, it is possible to have this level of deep relationship with others. Especially with the person of your choice who becomes a life partner. I suspect that you, like me, would never want to settle for anything less.

Heart connection with a life partner is absolutely beautiful. There is a flow of positive energy between these two hearts like no other experience. It is to be treasured and honed. It truly is a place where both feel highly honoured and held. In this place, there is no fear or control. Each feels that there is no depth of heart that cannot be shared. Everything within each heart can be transparent and open. No subject is censored because there is full exposure. This creates a huge vulnerability. But within that vulnerability, each heart is held, acknowledged, and heard. This, I believe, is the fullest expression of holding space for another.

Heart connection with one's life partner is so incredibly important. If you are in a position where you have yet to form this relationship, I believe what we are going to share next will help shape your understanding and help clarify and deepen your thoughts. For those of us who have a life partner, this may cause you some pain on reflection which requires some working through. The beauty of being in a sisterhood, as we aspire to be, is that we support each other in each of our life spaces and the challenges we find there.

The relationship we seek as heart-connected women needs to be (for our sake) with a partner who is on this same journey of his or her own. A truly awakened woman or an awakening one who is turning her face and heart to tune in to the universe needs a life partner who is able, understanding, and strong enough to hold her in that space. A heart-connected life partner needs to be able to demonstrate the following qualities.

- To be able to hear our dreams, visions, and ideas and support them and facilitate them without dismissal or ridicule or disapproval
- To have a divine purpose of his or her own, or seeking to find and develop it
- To be open about how the person is growing spiritually and to have open conversations about it with us

In other words, are these life partners able to share their hearts to the level and depth we are firing up in our own hearts? If not, is there is some fear? If we were to begin talking about these things with them, how would that feel? Could we do that without any resonance of fear? If not, it suggests that we are not truly heart connected to this person, nor can we be. They are not in the right place—yet.

This will, in time, cause an imbalance of the relationship. One we need to decide if we can commit or remain committed to. The choice is always hard. For some of us, it may mean letting the person go. If he or she cannot, will not, and does not hear your heart at any level, does one even have a relationship with that person anyway?

You see, a heart-connected union becomes a sacred container. It literally holds divine purpose and grows it synergistically (the idea that 2 + 2 = .6). The growth is amazing because the union is completely powered up. It has fire under its feet. I'm sure each of us wants to be in a power relationship like that. Awesome.

Once we have that, the power to stay faithfully and exclusively committed to each other is birthed. It is the true

## Divine Purpose

definition of marriage, I believe, when we think that through. It is laughable and even ridiculous to consider that this can be created by the signing of a legal document, a marriage certificate, to confirm such things. A true partnership occurs at the heart level and cannot be qualified by legalism.

Heart connection, although solid and beautiful, at the same time is fragile and delicate. It can be damaged. We need to remember that because the universe operates outside the construct of time, the elements of its expression, such as heart connection, also operate outside of time. It is then a moment by moment affair. Relationships are living, breathing entities with their own flavours and personalities. It is the heart connection that must be constantly pursued. Filled with love, light, and life. If not, it will wither and die. We all instinctively know this to be true.

There is nothing quite like the heart connection between mother and young child. The symbiosis is incredible. That bond exists even though the umbilical cord is cut at birth. Somehow, mother and baby seem completely in tune with each other. This is a perfect example of heart connectedness. It is, of course, necessary on an evolutionary basis for the survival of the baby. When my daughter was just two years old or so, I found it incredible that she spoke something I was thinking at exactly the same moment. It's almost supernatural. Spooky and natural at the same time. It occurs, I believe, because of the level of heart connectedness we were experiencing. That's an indicator of this flow at work.

Heart-connected souls know what each other are thinking and feeling at any given moment. For the really intuitive, they may also be able to discern physical pain in the other.

So to want and desire this heart connection in a

relationship with a life partner is all important. Dear sister, you and I deserve nothing less.

To be heart connected into a sisterhood is truly remarkable. Throughout our journey of exploring divine purpose together, we'll really get to embrace what that means for us. We're going to find that the need for connection and the gathering of sisters become ever more prevalent in our lives. We will get to the point where we just can't go without the heart-connected input of the sisterhood. The rest of this book explains why and how this should be. In the same way that the universe waits for us to respond with an expression of love as it pours out love to us, so do our sisters. We are intended to be gathered, united in that space of being together, standing and rising with the full awareness of what it is the universe has gifted each of us. There we have the power to be the universal expression of the life force itself. You see, it's in our union as sisters that we have the power to change our world. When we are heart connected with our sisterhood and the universe simultaneously, there is world-changing power.

Bring it on, sister.

**CHAPTER 3**

# *Three Feminine Superpowers*

> Ohh, I don't think you'll ever know a woman quite like me …
>
> Diana Prince as Wonder Woman, c1977

Our superpowers are given to us by the universe for one reason, and one reason only: to breathe life into people, places, situations, projects, and everything that we may encounter. It is the spiritual equivalent of the Midas touch. They are pure feminine gold.

Inside each of us beautiful girls, we hold superpowers in our hearts. We sisters have at least one superpower, although, we have the capacity to have them all. We are truly awesome.

These amazing superpowers are part of who we are; our personalities ride on them. They are truly gifts from the

## Rachel White

universe direct to our hearts so that we may flow as well-functioning feminine beings. They are the foundation of our divine purpose. Knowing and understanding how these superpowers flow in and out, curving, intertwining with our feminine essence, helps us better understand what the universe has gifted to us as our divine purposes.

So let's get to know them. I'm completely confident that you will identify with at least one. The way they operate within our hearts is that we are both drawn to our superpowers and urged to express them at the same time. When we take a closer look, we see that something even deeper occurs. These superpowers flow together and weave in, out, and between external and internal expressions of who we are. It's an internal, sacred essence of us at our cores, a connectivity between us and all that breathes life outside us. In our daily experiences, moment to moment, our superpowers keep us grounded.

So here they are.

- Creativity
- Intuition
- Healing

Here's the question for right now: Which one draws you? Which is the one that you can identify with the most? This is your major feminine superpower.

Precious sister, our superpowers are present inside us all the time. They've been deep within us all along. But for some, they have been squashed down so deep we fail even to recognise them for what they are. Acknowledgement has been dangerous! These superpowers have brought persecution and ridicule. Our mothers told us what their mothers told them, and their mothers told them going back

## Divine Purpose

centuries. Being a healer will get you accused of witchcraft; being intuitive will bring trouble. People won't understand. It's too much. People will wonder, *Who does she think she is, displaying her cleverness in her creativity?* On and on and on. Sound familiar? It's an unspoken no until we give ourselves permission to say yes. So here it is, our big, fat yes! Our permission to rekindle this fire.

It's long overdue. It's time to reclaim them, starting with our recognition and acknowledgement of what is currently already in our hearts. If we are honest, we are amazing in these areas. Just look inside and see it.

Our superpowers are the basis of our feminine essence, so what we really need to do is hook into our superpowers and find ways to honour ourselves in and because of them. Find ways to develop and expand them. Grow it large! As we do, we will find that our femininity grows within us. We will literally rise. Isn't that exciting? I've proven to myself in my own journey that when we become mindful of our superpowers and thus, the true nature of the power we hold, the feminine energy inside us almost tangibly jumps right out of our spirits and into other people. They can *feel* us.

A little while ago, as I worked with these thoughts, growing my feminine and connecting with nature, I walked down a street holding a lavender bud. I caressed it, smelling and really feeling a joy at being present with it. A man on the other side of the road shouted to me, "Hey, lady, I can feel your energy from over here." I truly believe in that moment (and whether he was hitting on me or not doesn't matter), he felt something in my energy he couldn't really explain. That's the power we have, girls. This is how it is, the feminine essence literally rising out of us.

That's really what it's all about—rising and raising our feminine essence. In order to do that effectively, we have to know how this plays out in the universal sense. How does this mysterious energy connection work?

The answer is simple yet profound. It starts with our hearts being open to receive everything that the universe has set for us. Everything we are going to discuss in this book, I know this will help us see in a new kind of clarity. This is the message I feel the universe has asked me to birth in all our hearts. It's time to know these deep mysteries.

The amazing thing is that when we are gathered and raised up as a sisterhood, standing alongside each other, we find that these superpowers are very evident amongst us in equal measure. We will be wonderful inspirations and resources for each other. We will see in each of us these superpowers at work in us all.

Fair to say that the feminine has been squashed, squeezed out of us over many centuries. Recognising our superpowers, turning them up to the max, reclaims our feminine! Read that again; it's profound. Put another way, our superpowers help us to rise as feminine female beings. Awesome!

So let's bring it on, sister. Are you ready? I am.

*Creativity*

We are designed to be creative. To create. To grow, to birth. To make something functional and beautiful. To shape beauty for beauty's sake. To feel pleasure at the work of our hands, the movement of our bodies, or the noise we can make. To acknowledge, admire, honour, hold.

There are two basic types of creativity. The likelihood is that we will flow and blend these types within ourselves. Most women are creative in some or many ways. However, there are some amongst us who really do power up their

## Divine Purpose

soul on this superpower. You go for it, sister. It's all good. It's everything you are designed to be as a gift from the universe.

The first basic type of creativity involves using one or more of our five senses to create items for beauty, functionality, or pleasure. Some of these things may include,

- Dance, moving your body to music however you choose
- Arts and crafts of all types
- Musicianship, creating, playing music from its source
- Singing and/or public speaking, using your voice to express yourself
- Painting/sculpting/drawing sewing/knitting, and so on.
- Writing and drawing, communicating, expressing ideas
- Photography/interior design
- Preparing food, using our senses of smell and taste in the environment
- Developing beautiful living and working spaces which maximise productivity and comfort
- Pregnancy and birth, bringing forth new life

There really is no limit to the list. Anything that's not on this list that you can creatively come up with is fabulous.

Some of us have natural talent in some of these areas. So our commitment to self is to explore and develop what we are naturally good at for our pleasure and for that of others. If we can create a business opportunity—which may or may not be appropriate—even better. It's super-authentic to feed our souls and provide financially for our needs through the use of elements of our creativity. The challenge is that we explore and develop our creativity in ways that we are not so familiar with. Maybe join a club or do a course. Really work on bringing this aspect of our feminine to the top. It's all good, and there's no limit. So just go for it.

The second type of creativity is a little more subtle but powerful and effective. This concerns the ability to use our skills in communication and thinking to facilitate, resolve, negotiate, and so on through interpersonal relationships. It takes a huge amount of creativity to see what precisely is needed in a situation and be able to implement it. Women are equipped way better than men, for example, to help a toddler through a tantrum or to see both sides of an issue between colleagues at war. To know what to say and what not to say in the heat of the moment. To diffuse anger in others, or sometimes provoke it in order to get to the raw truth. To see potential and communicate whatever is needed to help facilitate the birthing of that new thing. We have the power to creatively listen and to hold our sisters in distress. We can use creativity to know when to intervene and when not to. It's essential too in setting our boundaries to make situations win-win for everyone in the mix where we can. To think on our feet. To be diplomatic, acquiring what we want or need without force or demand or creating offense or distress in the other person. Of course, this level of creativity overlaps into our intuitive superpower. It is truly outstandingly awesome.

Everything about the feminine weaves, flows, and overlaps.

Creativity is essential to our feminine souls. We can't help but be given resources and grow them, expand, create, breathe life into them. It is the essence of that which the feminine is all about. It is the way in which we relate on a highly spiritual basis to the universe. Remember, the

## Divine Purpose

universe is full of love and light and life. So as we mindfully develop our own creativity, we are naturally aligning with the universe that does exactly the same thing. Growing, expanding, giving, breathing life.

A beautiful example came to me as I was writing this. This is exactly how the universe works; it puts people and circumstances in our paths, in our faces, pretty much to help us in our understanding right at the right moment. A mother at my son's special needs school slumped down in the reception area where I was waiting. As we've chatted before, I asked how she was. She had a huge ziplock bag and tipped the entire contents out onto the coffee table. There in front of us were sets of necklaces and earrings, other bits of jewellery made out of ribbons and buttons, and many quirky items that she had made. As we got talking, she shared with me how she makes jewellery at night as a stress reliever. Her son does not sleep well, and she needs to be up to watch him. Whilst she does, she uses her creativity to make these wonderful items. She was bringing them to school to sell to raise funds in her own small way. I was so touched, so moved. My darling, this is the power of creativity. It is a win-win. This woman is using her creativity to channel her feelings, tiredness, frustration, and emotional pain at caring for a special needs son and then gifting it so others can benefit. This is just one example of what this superpower is capable of; there are thousands more. The underlying message to our souls is that when we recognise this for what it is, honour, and acknowledge it, it is gift to ourselves, an investment with huge returns in a spiritual context.

I guarantee that as we pursue our creativity, the universe will reward our hearts richly with a full-up-ness. It is an excellent way for women to begin to deal with the sometimes empty feelings our hearts can contain. Creativity, or being creative in whatever context, is the opportunity to express the creativity of the universe ourselves. We have been entrusted with bringing life, restoring souls through beauty and comfort, and providing a calmness when others are struggling. Once we understand this, its power delves deep within our hearts. We are able to look at the entirety of our tasks and the work of our hands in a new way. If we can see this as both a gift and the expression of the universe inside and outside us at the same time, I know for sure we will have plugged our hearts into a power source and turned up the dial.

Because the universe is a life-giver and life-bringer, we have been highly honoured as the ones to conceive, nurture, and carry new life in our bodies until the day we can birth that baby into the world. It is truly awesome and somewhat a mystery to look at your body an hour after birthing and wonder, *How?* However, there is also deep pain associated with the longing to be able to birth. Some of us have not been able to conceive. Others have, for their own heartfelt reasons, terminated their pregnancies. Still others have had miscarriages, stillbirths, and cot deaths. All these produce pain in their own ways. The reason in part, I believe, is because we understand that our bodies have been chosen to bring life and to nurture it when it's here. But for whatever reason, it hasn't worked out that way. Or maybe we have the longing but not the right partner. Or maybe we just know that having a baby is not and never will be right for us. Or the circumstances are just the way that they are. I too lost three babies in utero, so I stand alongside my sisters in full awareness of this pain. It is a very deep pain of the feminine, and a woman who has this experience needs the love of her sisters, to be held, and the freedom to express it however she chooses. The pain of loss is also a form of creativity. Out of

## Divine Purpose

our losses, passion is born—passion for ourselves, passion for a cause, passion that we do everything in our power not to have another woman experience what we had no choice in experiencing. In fact, true passion can only come out of a place of loss. Are you beginning to see now how the feminine is designed to turn around every circumstance and creatively breathe the life force of the universe into it? See how it works. This is what it is all about. Our glorious feminine.

I want to share with our hearts really clearly that having a baby doesn't make us more feminine, just as not having one doesn't equate us with being less feminine. The world puts pressure on us to "deliver" the goods, literally. So I would like us to be able to reframe this idea. We agree that true femininity resides in our hearts, not in the womb. I know this is true. I have a girlfriend born without a womb, but she sure has a heart and is all woman. So none amongst us should feel lesser because of this issue. Instead, let's do the heart work to make us strong, aligning with the universe and our creativity superpower in every variation of any way we can to explore this in ourselves.

We are plugging into creativity because the universe that sent us has embedded creativity into us. It is creativity to be pursued in an adventurous, sacred way. Rather than mere childbirth, which is only an expression.

If you are like me, I'm sure you won't know a single woman who is not creative in some form or another. This creative force—this life force—is deeply planted in the feminine soul. It is like lifeblood to us as it is one of our feminine superpowers. Our challenge is to recognise how we are being creative in and through our lives and to honour it, develop it, expand it, and grow it. Frame it.

On our *Divine Purpose* Facebook page, Morgan, one of

our admins, asked the following question. It's one for our journal time for sure.

> My question for us all is, how are you intentionally creative? What are the things you do to express your feminine?

May I challenge our hearts to really detail this in a deep way? Come, sister, share this precious life-giving, affirming superpower with us on our *Divine Purpose* Facebook page. Help inspire the sisterhood to grow.

*Intuition*

Intuition is that simple knowing that you know that you know, a knowledge of inner things unsaid that are felt, known.

Intuition is our second feminine superpower. It's super-important. Some of us are highly skilled in this superpower, others not so. But wherever you find yourself, it is okay, more than okay, to just be.

Intuition serves many purposes. And as you would expect, it certainly overlaps with our other superpowers. It is a really powerful, special, and dangerous gift from the universe. But it is also highly prized and necessary.

When we think about it, it's been common parlance for centuries now for people to refer to "female intuition". It is a very real yet misunderstood power we hold right in the core of our feminine souls. I believe every woman has the power to tune in and access her own intuition. In reality, what's happening here is because we are expressions of the feminine within the universe. We are easily able to tap into that life-giving, breathing energy that exists in the universal sense. We can tune into, connect with, and decode it in such a beautiful, natural way.

## Divine Purpose

We must remember that intuition, as the energy of the universe, is all about love and light and life. When we connect with this and bring it out, it is always to be used for good purposes. Never evil or to cause harm. Of course, there are those who have the gift but not the maturity to apply it wisely. But for those of us on a journey of the heart, this is absolutely essential. Remember, the energy we are connecting with is "life bringing", so our application of intuition needs to be always grounded very solidly with the pure intention of being life affirming.

Imagine if you are able to have a knowing that someone is in physical pain without the individual telling you so in words. We may well be able to read pain and distress on the face. This is the basis for intuition. It is indeed quite easy for humans to decipher emotions displayed by facial expressions. The intuitive nature takes this a stage deeper. It is possible to know when someone maybe in emotional distress and yet masking it. As women, we can tune in to the full emotional spectrum of people around us. For sure, a beautiful training ground is through small children, who have no words and yet communicate their distress and needs non verbally. If mothers were completely devoid of this ability, their children would be at huge risk of neglect, starvation, and death. So we can see in a very real sense the purpose of intuition is to breathe life. To keep life going. Intuition is incredibly important.

Of course, this superpower extends far beyond utilising non-verbal communication with children before the age they can offer accuracy and descriptions of their inner worlds. Used purposefully, we can know when someone is being dishonest with us. We can sense the predator personality or the bad vibes. The discernment of evil and evil intent issuing from some people we encounter, the anger, and so on. What a beautiful protection this provides. When our intuition tells us, our gut feeling instructs us, no, always listen to it. In my experience, that feeling is never wrong.

Intuition helps us form healthy boundaries. The deep sense of knowing that we know that we know can help us to work out what is right for us, what we like, what we don't like and then to implement that. It helps us decide what we will tolerate (or not) in the actions of others towards us.

This is the superpower that helps us cut to the chase. With its help, we can call others out, help them see their inauthenticity, and to face their personal responsibility towards becoming more authentic. We can also tell the beautiful, heart-driven soul and feel drawn to this person as their energy matches ours.

Intuition can be dangerous. Calling time on inappropriate, unwanted, and toxic behaviours from others sometimes produces negative reactions. When we outline and reinforce our boundaries, if we are not resolved in our own hearts, it can make us feel wrong for bringing it to attention. An immature heart will always seek to make the other wrong for implementing boundaries. Our intuition helps us discern all these things and to examine the possible motivations of others when we realise that their hearts and resultant behaviours delight in evil.

Unfortunately, this is the one superpower that over the centuries has been squashed out of us. And no wonder. When we stand in its full force, we are, without words, asking for another's heart to change. That is a huge deal for the unawakened soul. So we would be wise to flow in compassion and without judgement in equal measure with our intuition in order for its application to be realised in a holistic, life-affirming way. Intuition is the superpower we most readily ditch in the face of fear or misunderstanding.

## Divine Purpose

The reasons for this are very valid. It is definitely a, "Handle with care and responsibility," superpower.

Let's take a moment to breathe and connect with our ancestor sisters and those around the world who have endured serious persecution and lost their lives because of intuition, the knowledge of knowing in the unseen realm. Let's reclaim this very special superpower as our own. Seek it with all wisdom; utilise it effectively and safely. Intuition is like a heavy, sharp sword. Used without training, support, and wisdom, it has the power to cut us in half instead of its proper purpose of defending us.

In reality, a woman without intuition, or one who denies it in herself, is a mere shell. She presents herself before the universe as a female being experiencing life only on a skin-deep level. Surviving, existing in chunks of living from one task she has to achieve to the next. Nothing is wrong with that. But do you want more and to live deeply? I sure do.

Turning on intuition, or deepening it, is really all about connecting our hearts to a range of emotions. It's about not allowing any fear in, being free to feel everything. This makes every emotion completely valid. At its fullest force, intuition reveals itself in the empathic connection we have with the energy of others. We may find ourselves knowing things about their lives in quite some detail that they have not spoken to us of. Lots of women like to use props and tools to help with this level of connection. This is where we get the idea of using stones, cards, astrology, and so on, to help us connect and receive messages for others from the universe. My personal feeling is that as the universe put everything inside us as women, we have all the power resources we need. No props required.

Intuition is sometimes also able to see into the future. Not necessarily crystal-ball gazing, but just a deep sense of inner knowing and feeling. Some women have this so strongly; the universe communicates to them in dreams, visions, and premonitions. We have to remember that the universe operates outside our construct of time and space. Therefore, when we plug in, we attune to the source, as it were, where we can see things that have happened in a different space-time continuum to our present reality. There are some amongst us so gifted that they are able to locate missing children, and work out the clues in unsolved criminal cases, and these kinds of things. There are others who are gifted in hearing from the universe on behalf of others. We sometimes refer to that as being able to read people. Women with an intuitive superpower are often able to do this with great depth and accuracy. It comes through to them very naturally as a feeling or a sensation. Beautiful as it is, intuition is rooted in our hearts with empathy, compassion, and a very solid sense of emotional intelligence. Working to extend our intuition includes softening our hearts to receive and encompass these attributes.

Remember our chapter on heart connection? This fits beautifully when we realise that the gift of intuition is a heart-connectedness to the emotional energy around us. The superpower element comes in our abilities in knowing how to handle it and to use what is presented in that energetic field to promote life. Which, of course, may be some form of healing, restoration of relationship, to bring peace to a situation, or as we said before, to facilitate protection. Which leads us very well to our third feminine superpower.

*Healing*

What an amazing superpower. We have been so damped down that our twenty-first-century minds consider that healing comes pretty much only when we visit the doctor or

## Divine Purpose

hospital and receive treatment and medications. Whilst true, what an incredibly narrow viewpoint that is. The feminine is well suited to bringing healing/restoration to the body, the mind, to situations, to relationships. In essence, "restoration" is a far better word to describe what we mean here.

Essentially, bringing healing and restoration is about bringing our softness into a situation. We already know this instinctively. This is not news to us. As women, we can use our softness to provide a depth that is unique to us; men can't. Again, that softness brings and breathes life into all whom we touch, all who comes across our paths.

We have this amazing superpower to explore and develop what restoration—or being restored—means on a very deep level. It is literally world changing on its own.

Physical healing is wonderful. In ancient times, wise women were the keepers of the wisdom to know which plants and herbs could be used as remedies for ailments, how to treat a body with open wounds, and so on, to prevent further infection, disease, and ultimately, death. Of course, these women were also very involved in midwifery in their community or tribe and had a lot of experience and skill. The mysteries of these healings were not well understood. To a deadened heart and soul, preserving life in the face of death or bringing new life into the world is like magic. For centuries, women have been persecuted as though practicing witchcraft—invoking the power of the devil—because of this knowledge. Imagine then a woman with this power of healing and restoration; many are sustained and recovered through her touch and application of her knowledge. However, in holding the power, a well-loved person in the community dies. (Death does come to all.) The wise woman with this power is at risk of being accused of casting spells or bringing on a curse. Either way, it seems she cannot win. She is blamed and shamed in her feminine power. Her superpower in healing is completely misunderstood. Such a woman risks her life to bring healing through her superpower.

I am not surprised that many women in history continued in the face of persecution as their self-belief was strong. They understood that feminine essence, expressed through their superpowers and grounding them in their divine purpose, had to be their top spiritual priorities. They were completely drawn in and focused on their purpose for living. Fantastic! In modern times, the whole scientific elements of medicine, surgery, and the criteria for being a doctor in a medical field have been completely commandeered by men, systems, and logical applications. We sisters have travelled a long, difficult journey to be healers and restorers.

The most important thing to realise is that restoration begins as energy work. See how it flows and overlaps with intuition. By tuning in to our universe of pure love, we become conduits of its flow. This is the biggest secret of all. Fear and death cannot coexist in the same place as love and life.

This is why many of us already know instinctively that to hold someone in life-affirming ways makes all the difference. Whether that be through physical hugging, deep listening to their pain, or meeting the challenge of a physical need, like providing a woman safe passage or shelter or resources to escape an abusive situation. All these things, as well as many others, bring healing—restoration—in their own contexts.

Sister, if you have this superpower, I urge you to develop it through the use of energy work, counselling, befriending, anyway that you can. If you are called to study medicine and become a doctor, nurse, or midwife, that is brilliant. But there is so much more in this arena. It may even be

## Divine Purpose

as simple as a smile and wink to a mischievous child if the parent is overwhelmed at his or her normal behaviours. Understanding the power of touch, using and studying alternative practices, and the simple knowledge that the presence of our feminine energy and our wisdom from our hearts have the power to help restore someone's broken soul.

It is incredibly powerful to use our healing/restoration superpower. Our feminine hearts constantly tug us in this direction to be world-changers with our gift of healing. Imagine if we were able to gift a precious sister into freedom and safety with the resources the universe has gifted us, money, time, knowledge, and a clear sense of what to do next. To help her have clarity, wisdom in her situation. Well, for that one woman, her children, and very possibly the legacy of her grandchildren and all who come after her, we will have changed their world for all time. Can we see the power that this has?

One of our beautiful Facebook girls, Mally, posted the following when I was writing this. As she did, my spirit jumped. "As a healer you will see ALL things as ONE OF THESE: LOVE or A CALL FOR LOVE."

Absolutely. This is the bottom line, isn't it? This is the call. It's all about love and how we communicate what the universe has given us as a superpower of healing, which is love, an expression of that pure love.

There are times when we need to use boundary setting to help us help another. Sometimes, oftentimes, being wise enough to give our superpower without limitation is amazing. At the same time, facilitating others to find their own power means we leave room and space for them to pick up the tab of their own adult responsibilities. Wisdom is key here. I believe as we explore our journey with our superpowers that the universe will hand us an equal measure of wisdom.

These are precious gifts. The heart-humbling thing is that we can't really misuse them if we stay aligned to the source that provides. But care is always needed.

My darling girl, it is likely then you will be able to identify within your spirit one superpower that you major in. I'm hopeful that on reading this through, clarity will pop into place. and you will know yourself better. This superpower is your gift from the universe for you to dwell in, magnify, and give back to the universe as your gift to the world from a pure heart.

My calling as an empowerer is to say, "Just go for it." Expand your superpowers in any amazing ways that you can think of. Really hone your skills in that area, and get immersed in it. Excellent heart work would be to come out of the comfort zone and develop abilities in other areas also, so that your feminine has a flavour of it all. They all overlap anyway.

Journaling this journey would be helpful so that in time, you can look back and see how far you've come. And, of course, come and share that with us on our *Divine Purpose* Facebook page.

The feminine essence comes right out of our superpowers, so don't hold back on any of it. We need them to be able to change the world. That is why they have systematically been squashed down and out of us for centuries. We need our superpowers to lay a foundation for our own unique divine purpose. When we awaken to how powerful we truly are and begin to reclaim what is rightfully ours, we will literally rise!

# CHAPTER 4

# *Our Ancient Ancestor Sisters*

The more a daughter knows the details of her mother's life—the stronger the daughter.
    —Anita Diarmant, *The Red Tent*

Humans have primarily lived in tribes or communities for most of our existence. Our experiences of living in urban town spaces, not really working with or even knowing people living around us, is a very modern phenomenon. Although our evolution and advances in science and technology are fabulous in many ways, they have also produced a backward step, a de-evolution in our social, community, heart connectedness across the human race. Everything we do in the Western world particularly is well boxed. Everything happens in a box—home, job, transport, even family; our buildings and transport are even box shaped. That's producing a problem in the female psyche I believe. The feminine is like a river, flowing, weaving, curving. We truly do live in a male-orientated, nine-to-five construct of a world. We are made to or feel like we should fit. No wonder the feminine essence is not at full power. No wonder more women than men are diagnosed with clinical depression. No wonder women feel they must do everything just to be on an equal footing with men. We even tend to eat male-sized portions because that's what's served up to us in restaurants (not surprising some of us struggle with our weight), and we sit in standard-made chairs and can't comfortably put our feet flat on the floor. I can't even work out how the TV remote works. Made by males from a male perspective. We have got to change some things.

Our ancestors had a far different experience. Our ancient sisters lived in a tight female community and had sister support surrounding them 24/7. In the nomadic tribes, male and female roles were clearly defined. Whilst in our modern hearts, we object to the seat of patriarchy of their societal organisations. In their time, it was accepted and normal, a clear part of their daily experiences. I believe the women of the tribe made the very best of that and used it to their advantage as far as they were able to. The male role was very much one of provider, hunter, protector. The female role focused on birthing, nurturing, and healing. (See how this fits into our feminine superpower we talked about in the last chapter?) Women in these tribes relied very heavily on each other, especially when the men were away from camp, hunting food. It was commonplace for the tribe to erect a red tent which served a very special purpose. Very likely, this tent was set some distance away, on the edge of the camp. It truly was a women-only space.

The red tent was where women would go to be in labour

## Divine Purpose

and give birth. It would have been a safe, private, clean(ish), comfortable place and somewhat sacred. With a recognised member of the company of women, an experienced older wise woman, very possibly as an early form of midwife.

The red tent served other purposes too. A young woman would be prepared for her marriage or betrothal ceremony from within the tent. And it was a place where any woman could go in time of crisis. The feminine was celebrated here in its purest form. A ceremony or ritual was performed when a young girl started menstruating. Welcoming her into the community of women now also able to reproduce was regarded in high importance. We, of course, don't know what that ceremony of celebration involved, but we can be sure it was acknowledged in the life of the blossoming woman. A beautiful recognition of menarche, the start of menstruation. Once a woman finished her menstruation for good and entered menopause, that was also recognised within the red tent with some sort of acknowledgement that she was now a wise woman, a crone; I prefer the term "wise woman"). Every stage in a woman's life was honoured and recognised.

It was an almost legal thing under biblical patriarchy that women were set apart at the time of their periods. In other words, she couldn't stay at home in her tent with her man, even if she—or he—wanted her to. Unfortunately in that time, a bleeding woman was seen as unclean. We find that abhorrent, and it has no place in our hearts today. Consider, though, that women living in a tribe together would all menstruate at the same time, all have PMT at the same time, and all ovulate at the same point each month. If all women were required to leave the family dwellings at this time, they would all gather in the red tent together, usually at the time of the full moon. It's so easy to see that they would gather for three days and nights to celebrate and hold each other. How amazing that must have been. I'm quite sure there were special rituals, cleansing ceremonies, crying, and singing together as well as the sharing of food and creativity. Women had to enter the red tent; they had no choice. What an amazing space.

It also served as protection. A woman physically beaten by her man (or anyone) would enter the red tent. He would not be allowed to hide her away. Well, her bruises were seen by the entire sisterhood, and her story told in tears. He could not get away with that. The matter was taken to the elder of the tribe for the offender/abuser to be dealt with.

What an amazing place to be gathered with your sisters for a once-a-month retreat. Only babies at the breast could enter with their mothers. Other children could not.

Once a young woman began menstruating, she was of marriageable age as she was able to reproduce. This was the expectation in these ancient communities. Again, we find this uncomfortable to consider twelve- or thirteen-year-old girls marriageable. But at this time in history, it was accepted. Generally, people didn't live as long; not too many lived past their fiftieth year. So their perceptions, experiences, and expectations were different than ours.

There is so much we can learn from our ancient sisters. This concept of being gathered together is something we have lost, and we miss it dearly without even realising it as it is centuries beyond our experience.

I find it incredibly sad that women all over the world sit on their sofas during their period month after month feeling urggh, maybe with cramps, highly emotional, feeling vulnerable to all sorts of emotional triggers after a normal day of working to serve others in whatever capacity. Often feeling overwhelmed and having no sisterly company. Instead, enjoying the companionship of a grumpy man (as he knows he likely won't get sexual pleasures for a few days, maybe a week), who doesn't understand and cannot be expected to. Or she might be sitting all alone. I find that a tragedy. All alone with her internal world, one way or another. She, I, and you need a gathered and raised sisterhood for support in such moments.

We need each other more than we even know. Not many of us were celebrated on starting our menstruation. I certainly wasn't. Our common collective experience consists of having its mechanics and how to deal with it explained by an equally embarrassed mother. Some of us aren't even that lucky. It all contributes to a feeling that to be female and to consider the amazing job our bodies do and are capable of is somehow wrong, taboo. Whilst I'm not a proponent of free bleeding all over the place just because it's natural, I feel that there does need to be balance and acknowledgement. Being female, having this body, and celebrating all that it is capable of is very much needed. Therefore, missed by most of us in our lives. No wonder we've come to see it as a curse, a painful inconvenience.

Sisters, we simply must find a way to celebrate and acknowledge *all* of ourselves. Every part. Squashing down the feminine most certainly occurs when we stand in embarrassment or shame about the natural functions of our bodies. We spend over thirty years of our lives secretly menstruating, worrying about leaking, feeling rough every week in four. If we are going to reclaim our feminine, this is a huge aspect.

I propose that we modern women find a way to gather together regularly to celebrate the feminine, to rejoice with each other, to hold each other. Sharing our hearts. Giving our wisdoms to our daughters and young maidens, to pick up and pass on the baton of what it is to be truly feminine in every aspect of us. Yes, our glorious female nature needs to be nurtured, cherished, adored. What better place to celebrate and acknowledge our feminine superpowers, find our truth in our divine purpose, and cry our tears than in the laps of our precious sisters?

It is our coming together, our being with each other, and celebrating our feminine that is most important. This is what we must reclaim in order to rise. In later chapters, we explore these themes in more depth.

*Author's Note*

Around the world, a red tent movement is growing. Why not investigate how to join with a local expression of the red tent movement? Or better still, start your own.

Through our *Heart Maidens* Facebook page, we run our own version of the red tent. You are very welcome to attend.

## CHAPTER 5

# *Empowerment*

If all are equal, then no one is truly your superior or inferior.
—Rik Mayall (UK comedian), 1958–2014

For sure the universe has called me to be an empowerer. It is definitely my divine purpose. Fair to say, though, that empowerment in my life and heart is completely birthed out of its total opposite—oppression. I went through an awakening in order to understand what empowerment is all about.

Empowerment in its essential form is all about permission giving and the power of choice. Then it is followed by the provision of resources to make things happen, so deep inside us we can feel and own the motivation to say to hearts, "Let's go. Let's get on this thing." Empowerment is the ending of oppression at every level and in every context. In order to fully understand empowerment, we must come to understand what oppression is so that our hearts can understand the bigger picture.

"Oppression" literally means to stand against. How many times in our female experience, in our human experience, do we find that others have completely stood against us in big and small ways? Deliberate, covert, hidden. In all sorts of ways, oppression can rear its ugly head. Oppression often produces a significant outcome of invalidation, identifiable through the inner resonance or sensation in our solar plexus.

Oppression takes away our power to choose for ourselves. As an adult, anytime we see someone making choices for our bodies, our money, our time, our voice and we have no choice, no ability to say no or to have our hearts heard, something is taken from us. This is oppression. It is a rape of the soul and deadens our hearts. The oppressor takes and takes, and leaves little to no room for our free will and our choices.

Remember, in our first chapter we talked about free will from the universe? The universe operates within the principle of pure love and light and life. It is the universe that sent us on that foundation of love into our earthly space. The universe allows us free will because, of course, that is what pure love is. There is no control, no limit on our hearts because if the universe did that, it would become our oppressor and not pure love any longer. It can only be one way or the other. We said that the universe longs for us to line our hearts up in response to its huge heart of love.

Being an oppressor—one who stands against and not for, with, or alongside—indicates an unaligned heart. Darling, are you beginning to see this with more clarity now? I hope so.

The oppressor never promotes the universe's value of pure love; it's impossible. Such a heart is after its own ends.

## Divine Purpose

It places itself on a dictatorial throne. It makes decisions for other people's lives or their actions in the moment that are not its to make—although it believes so out of its perception of entitlement. It rips choices and opportunities to be and to grow right out of the hearts of others. It squashes, crushes, seeks to make everything smaller and insignificant, and to destroy. Empowerment does the exact opposite, birthing, growing, nurturing, cultivating, acknowledging, growing big, rejoicing in the delight of others' achievements, and giving permission and positivity. All these are things we long for.

It is easy to see that we girls have had it tough, being informed what is and is not feminine from non-female beings. Like, how would they know anyhow? We have experienced abuses against our female bodies that were not our choice, being subjugated to second place, ridiculed for our different perspectives, controlled, dominated, manipulated. We've been made to feel too much and then again, not enough. And in the middle of it all are our beautiful feminine hearts just longing to be really heard, really seen, and really acknowledged. The ultimate price of oppression in its fullest form is death. Death to our souls and/or death to our bodies. We have to know what this oppression is in order to be able to rise.

An oppressor is a soul killer. We who are on a journey of the heart long to be and are life-givers. Again, two complete opposites. This is the basis of empowerment. As a concept, empowerment breathes life into situations, rekindles a dying fire, and gives permission. To recognise and endorse whatever it is that is good in another's heart, encouraging the person to go for whatever stirs one's passion.

Empowerment is essentially permission giving. It's standing alongside another and being for the other person as much as possible at every level. It is a go and a yes and a win. There are a couple of ways we can enhance this attitude in ourselves to become empowerers of others.

Create and endorse win-win situations. As women on heart journeys, there is simply no room for setting anyone up to fail. Everyone wins. This is incredibly important. Some people shy away from grasping this concept because of fear, a belief that helping another win somehow diminishes their own power. This is untrue. (I wish with all my heart our brothers would get this idea.) If we help another person to win at his or her thing, we also win because we've facilitated it and helped launch that person in to it. The winning/losing continuum is a very masculine construct. It is very hard for males to concede to their perceptions of losing. They are hardwired to always win. However, the female heart thrives on win-win. We have hearts fully equipped to give *and* receive, a win-win on an energy-exchange basis.

To create environments that promote life, we need clutter-free, tidy living spaces in order to move freely and power up to the best of our abilities. You see, if we are always chasing our tails trying to get straight and organised, we become survivors instead of thrivers. Stressed out by never finding anything, never being able to complete projects, exhausted from frustration, or from the frustration of others existing—surviving—in chaos.

We can create energetically enhanced environments that nourish our souls. This is what the practice of feng shui is all about. I believe that this is helpful for us here, but the most important is to develop clutter-free spaces and get clean and organised.

The beauty of a female heart is that beauty extends itself to our environments. We need our beauty to be reflected back at us in order to feel more beautiful. I've discovered this is important for my soul. For sure my levels of productivity and proactivity increase when I feel like the queen in pleasant surroundings. Because you are a queen, don't you deserve to live in a palace? Yes, yes. You do! Although maybe not an actual palace or even a mansion, it is your palace because you are the queen in it. Although not impossible, it's much harder to feel like the queen in our lives when we are contained up to our eyeballs in a disorganised fishbowl of mess and clutter. That extends to our emotional environment as well. If we have people around us who are chaotic or angry much of the time, it's not helpful to our feminine hearts of love and life. I feel more engaged, alive, involved, free, wild, and unrestricted when the environment feeds me positive energy. It's just as important to surround ourselves with positive people who invest in and nourish our souls. In reality, this is where the process of flow begins. Being aligned more authentically with and inside the universe is a powerful place to reside.

Empowerment, of course, comes when we know our divine purpose, are living in it, and are pursuing it. (We discuss this in depth in our chapter on divine purpose.)

We give away our power all the time. We do so primarily in two distinct ways. It's easy to assume that in giving our power to another depletes us. So logically, we conclude we need some sort of refill or to top up. In reality, the exchange of power should operate in a loop system. I give you some of my power to empower you, and you give me some power in return to empower me. But we know full well this rarely occurs. Whilst nice, it doesn't really work that way. That means when we come into the fullness of realisation about it, we have to be the ones who blaze this trail and model the concept with no expectations that it will be returned to us in that moment. We have to kick-start this somewhere. As we said before, empowerment or the process of empowerment is essentially permission giving. So right now, sister, I give you permission to be totally you in all your glory.

Someone quite wise once told me that if we, "Use our authority, we lose it." I believed that mantra for some time. However, my thoughts on this have shifted and deepened. I've realised for that statement to be true, we must first have authority over another. Spiritually speaking, in an exchange of pure love energy, this is not true because no one has more authority than another, and none is more superior or inferior than another. We are equal. It is only our perception that directs our thinking. Authority over others comes with the construct of rankings and hierarchy.

The first way we give away power is to allow people to *take* it from us—the doormat syndrome. We've all been there. We've done this to others, and we've for sure had others do it to us. That sense when we are in a relationship with another and inequality unbalances the scales. The energy exchange goes one way, with one person taking and one giving. When we look at this closely, we see a couple of things going on. The first is poor boundary setting.

Many of us get into this because we have been conditioned and trained to do so. This especially applies to us women. To give way, literally, to others all the time. To say yes when we mean no, and to say no when we mean yes. We've all been in this place, allowing people to behave in the most appalling ways to us and to just absorb all that poison. As a protection, maybe—to not make a fuss, to make it better (for them), or to save embarrassment. There are all sorts of justifications that we've used in the moment for not speaking our truth or standing up for ourselves. Most of which are rooted in fear. We've reacted badly and been defensive, vindictive, resentful, and revengeful. And we

## Divine Purpose

carried that baggage around for years. All of us have done that! I've done that. When we absorb all this poison on behalf of others, our hearts eventually become weighted with a sense of resentful pain and an almost strangling feeling of not even knowing what our choices—from a pure-hearted place—would even be. This is giving away our power big time again and again. And I have to tell you I'm the world's worst at doing this.

We need our sisterhood in these moments to hear and hold us, and get our hearts straightened out on this without judgement. This is a cornerstone of how we can rise together, helping us all to regain and reclaim the power that is rightfully ours—the power of mastery of self. Great boundary setting comes when we are clear about what we do and don't want. That's why it is essential as women to take time alone every day just to be with ourselves. Journaling is great for this. I'm always recommending it. Get a sparkly, expensive as you can afford (because you are worth it) notebook. Take it with you wherever you go. We are so used to doing for others all the time, we forget sometimes that we are even here. Until that crisis, that wobbly moment, the emotional crashing into a wall comes. And it always does. Without taking time to know our hearts and writing up our innermost thoughts on this and what our desires are, our preferences, boundaries, divine purpose. When that moment comes, we compromise, we go along with, we buckle under pressure, we feel weak all because we've not been true to ourselves. How can we be true to ourselves and stand in our own truths and their power if we don't check in with ourselves often enough to even know what that truth even is. Sister, I know I'm scratching where you are itching with these words. This is so important. Reclaiming our power and standing in it needs to be a daily practice.

## Rachel White

Our hearts need personal space, alone time to breathe and flourish. We can't carry on having our hearts and souls beat in time with everyone else all the time. The repercussion of it is deadly. Even that word, "re-percussion" is telling us. Beat a drum hard with two or more sticks at the same time for long enough, and the drum skin eventually breaks. It's totally the same with our gorgeous feminine hearts.

My darling, we cannot hope for one second to either receive empowerment from another or to give it in a pure-hearted way until we begin to look at how we sabotage our power all the time. To ensure that empowerment is effective, we must deal with our hearts at this level, raw and painful as it is: But super-necessary for growth. Otherwise, we are merely a bucket with a hole in it. Everything of value leaks out of us all the time.

Another way we lose our power is by being and remaining in victimhood. I know for sure there is not one amongst us who has not had bad things happen to our bodies and souls. Some of us have had extremely bad things happen which were not our choice, and they have given us great pain. I hear your heart, sister, and we will address this a little more in our chapter on the wounded feminine later in this book. For now, I want to speak very deeply into our hearts and say that we are not our pain or abuse. These terrible things have no place in defining our hearts. We give up our power because living inside the hurt, feeling it so intensely, keeping it alive (which is understandable, so there's no judgement here), leads to us making a spiritual kind of contract with it. Somewhere inside, we believe that it owns us. It has us in a firm grip. We know this because we can feel the resonance of that pain in our bodies (remember that emotional energy is a vibration) much of the time. It's always there in our thoughts our dreams, our responses, shaping

## Divine Purpose

how we view the world and others all the time. Within that energy exchange where we've kept the pain alive, we've given it our power. That's why we can see in our hearts and sometimes in others, people absolutely consumed by those negative feelings of hate, anger, revenge, and so on. It's as though the soul has now been taken over and possessed by these things. (Possession is to do with ownership.) Where as we, women on a journey of the heart, desire to be completely immersed and bathed in love and light and life, the values of the universe. In order to fly free into our divine purpose and to step into our rightful place, reclaiming our power we need to make a new agreement. The power of the universe that sent us from a place of love and light is bigger and stronger than any pain, any abuser, or any situation introduced into our hearts. In other words, pain, hurt, and abuse doesn't own us. Pure love itself does.

Make a new agreement with your heart that nothing and no one owns it except that love. This big love can be trusted to hold us. This is scary at first because we are so used to the pain. Like we talked about in our chapter on the universe, we believe the universe that loves us so should have protected us and prevented our suffering. Without remembering that the universe cannot go against the free will of others. This is a huge concept to get our heads around. It is a hard road to travel. Healing is here for us when we begin to understand the bigger picture. Please share with us as a sisterhood as you walk through this path on your journey. We are here to help each other grow.

We have far more power than we are aware of, certainly in my heart. Being an empowerer or a releaser of power into others is my assignment from the universe. I'm hopeful that what I'm sharing helps us to see what and where our personalised powers, given to us by the universe are, to facilitate and access them, and give permission to go with that flow. I know for sure that once we begin to take teeny-tiny steps in the direction of our divine purpose, having discovered what it may be, the commitment in moving towards it brings us to deeper alignment with the universe. The profound thing is that once we begin to do this, the universe itself begins to provide all the resources that we need in order to fulfil each step of the journey. There is never a need to panic about funds or the right people connections or resources we may need. Once alignment begins, everything falls into place. Now, sometimes there is a stalling. This simply means that the universe has other things to teach and to gift you beforehand. There is often preparation work to be done with our hearts, and this is okay. All we need do is trust. Unfortunately, our human minds can get in the way at this point, producing panic and fear and force, where we push the thing forward. Be careful to acknowledge that for what it is because fear and love can't coexist in the same space at the same time. Our beautiful alignment will be off centre if we push for it. So relax into this journey. It is much more of an embracement of our new realisations that we need to cultivate.

Do you see what our arms are doing differently? In embracing, we are gathering into the self; in pushing, we are actually rejecting that which has come along. This is the visual picture of the mindset we need in order to line up with the divine purpose the universe has ordained for us. The universe is holding you in pure love. So is the sisterhood. We need our sisters more than ever to be our empowerers, to give us permission to flow with the wildest calls of our hearts. Of course, we need to do that for each other. Be open to respond if the universe leads you to fund another sister into her freedom, to gift her a plane ticket, a meal, contacts,

## Divine Purpose

anything at all that makes it possible for her to be and do whatever it is the universe calls her into. This is the ultimate in permission giving.

I promise that as an empowerer I will stand with you on this journey. Petitioning the universe that we may all fully step in to our divine purpose.

# CHAPTER 6

# *Divine Purpose*

> The purpose of Divine Purpose is to expand and grow the universe. Our commitment and alignment to the process grows us and the universe in pure love.
> —Rachel White, *Divine Purpose*, 2019

Hurrah, we get to talking about divine purpose, the subject of this book. I really did leave it until now quite deliberately for a couple of reasons. First, I wanted our hearts to have a grounding in the things we discussed in our earlier chapters because divine purpose, in its fullness, comes out of these places. Also, it takes quite a mature heart (I don't mean old) really resolved to self to be able to grasp the concept of divine purpose. To be at the place in a spiritual sense in our lives to walk forward into whatever it is the universe has for us. It requires that we have journeyed along our paths sufficiently to be surrendered to the universe—the

## Divine Purpose

life force, a giver of life and breath—instead of us pushing or striving for things that are of little consequence in a spiritual context. It is the difference, some say, between operating in a low-vibrational or high-vibrational way. If we seek, let us seek things that the universe holds in the highest value. Let us learn its language of pure love and line right up with it. It is definitely for the strong-hearted. There are some women amongst us who are on deep healing journeys who may still be in survival mode or overcoming mode. That is okay. It's a necessary part of the journey. Regrouping our hearts and souls because of traumatic situations and things of that nature does need to be dealt with first. Dealing with divine purpose may not yet be your first priority. If that's the case, that's okay. You'll have other things to work through before you are ready to embrace fully your divine purpose. I want you to know that you are loved and held by the universe and our sisterhood. This is a stage of an exciting spiritual journey from darkness to light wherever you may find yourself.

Divine purpose is ... Well, we know that the divine is the sacred—some say God, some say the universe, our life force—in us, around us, outside us. All at the same time. "Purpose" means an assignment or mission, a calling. The universe has deliberately chosen us, you and I, to fulfil a very special mission, a calling unique for each of us. For this generation, this time, this *now*. We are conduits, if you like, through which the universe of pure love chooses to express itself to the world. To expand, birth and grow love and light and life. Isn't that incredibly awesome?

Divine purpose is the why and the what that the universe sent us here to do. Although it's more than a *doing*; it's *being*. We exist inside of it. We define it. At the same time, it defines us. The beautiful thing is that we get to choose what it is, whilst the universe has decided it too. As we align our hearts with the universe, there is no tension. It is all perfect. So no one needs to worry that they will be called to do something they don't want to do. Or that they might miss it. No, darling, if you seek it, it will find you. It is our precious universe that has placed and embedded that desire deep within our spirits before birth. Our job is now to wake up what is dormant, asleep within us, and to move. Flow with that flow.

Divine purpose comes right out of our feminine superpowers: creativity, healing, and intuition. Identifying where we sit with our superpowers is a great first step in coming to realise what our divine purpose truly is. It's gifted by the universe, and it's always going to be something that brings love and light and life. Our assignment is never going to be something horrid, abusive, or anything like that. I think that's important to note because at times, we are prone to letting our darker thoughts and egos run away with us. So in helping our hearts define what our divine purposes are, we need some clarity, some parameters so that our hearts don't lie to our spirits out of selfish ambition or gain.

The immature heart may say, "Well, my divine purpose is to be rich or to be famous or to have this or that material object, to be married or not." In other words, the underdeveloped attitude of accessing divine purpose from that place is all about personal gain. Those kinds of things. This is a huge misunderstanding. Divine purpose is a gift to our hearts. It has the flavour of the universe's values and not necessarily our human ones. Imagine that our divine purposes sit inside our hearts radiating outwards. It is all about projecting the universe, the sacred within us, outwards. Now think how that could possibly work with a car or a hot tub. Or a husband (nice as they are). Do you see what I mean here? Those things are about getting and

## Divine Purpose

gathering into ourselves. One's divine purpose operates the other way around. It's inside first, and each of us puts it out there; it is bigger than "stuff". It is the heartbeat of the universe itself. This is what makes it high value and of a higher vibration in a spiritual sense. It is the sacredness of the universe, expressing itself through our willingness, our surrendered heart, to hear its call. Our response is from the heart through our outward positive actions.

I know that the universe has called me to be an empowerer, a permission giver, one who facilitates a big yes in the hearts of others, one who leads others to their own understanding of what divine purpose means for them. The universe calls each one of us to our unique divine purpose.

The beautiful thing is that when we stand and rise together, each in the fullness of our divine purposes, we are able to change the world. I truly believe that. Imagine all over the world every beautiful sister (and brother, as this is not exclusively for us; the masculine heart applies it just a little differently), standing and rising in their full divine purpose power. Aligned with the universe, on track, doing, and being what they are called to do. Hatred, fear, rage, war, violence, patriarchy, abuse, and oppression of every kind cannot stand in the face of that.

That is why this is so important, sisters. Our alignment with the universe and each other in our divine purpose has real power. We have the power to change *everything*.

I know you want this. I can already hear your heart chiming with mine. It is so exciting and humbling. In our next chapter, we explore how we can be specific about it and help each of us find out what our own divine purpose is.

# CHAPTER 7

# *Your Divine Purpose*

> You were always there for me, the
> tender wind that carried me
> A light in the dark shining your love into my life.
> You've been my inspiration, through
> the lies you were the truth.
> My world is a better place because of you.
>
> —Diane Warren, "Because You Loved Me"

Your divine purpose is like a banner headline over the entirety of your life. It is bigger than our names and our status as a wife or mother or daughter or all three. It's bigger than our jobs, our careers, our faith or religions, our relationships, our talents, our community service. Bigger than it all. Like we said before, it defines us, and we define it at a soul level. The litmus test is when it is so ingrained in our lives and how we live it that other people notice and begin to use it as a definition of our values and characters

## Divine Purpose

when describing or referring to us. In other words, we become known for it.

Beautiful sister, I know you are ready to begin to know what your unique, handpicked gift from the universe, your divine purpose, is. We are ready. I stand with you, so for your journal, here is the big question.

What is my divine purpose; what is it that the universe is calling me to do or be?

This is a deep question, somewhere inside, your spirit knows the answer. It already lies within waiting to be recognised and resolved. Once we get clarity, everything in our lives start to fit into place in the most natural of ways.

This question and its answer are between you and the universe. I can't even begin to tell you what it may be. The universe will reveal it to you. It will come to you now in these next days as you are ready to receive it. Whilst we journey further together, I'll help with some input as much as I can. Come, gather with us online whilst you work this through. Knowing our divine purpose is so worth it. Finally, we get a sense—when it is resolved in us—that we know why we have been placed here. This sweet spot of recognition often produces an ecstatic jump in our hearts, our spirits as we finally get it. Our feminine becomes resolved. We understand that we have our divine purpose as a gift and mysteriously, we feel the need to gift it out of ourselves and back to the universe.

So here are some things that it could be. Remember, though, it is unique to you. Each of us get to define it in our own words.

- Peacemaker
- Truth teller
- Justice bringer

### Rachel White

- Trailblazer
- Empowerer
- Reconciler
- Birther/midwife
- Joy bringer

These are just a few examples. As we petition the universe, it will become clearer and clearer. Your divine purpose may not be on this list as it is personal, tailored to you. However, it will be a big-picture viewpoint. By that I mean it won't be detailed in its descriptive form. Not yet. It is a word, a definition that sits over your heart and soul and directs your footsteps into the detail as we begin to explore and unpack this more and more.

The first thing we need to do is identify what our unique divine purpose is. This may take some time. Start with spending time alone in nature with your journal. Detail a few things out, and let your thoughts flow. Nothing that comes to mind or that you write down will be wrong, so just get it all out there. Or speak your thoughts into your voice recorder of your phone.

Here are some pointers.

- What values from the universe am I most passionate about?
- What evils/oppressions do I see in my world that particularly gets me very upset?
- Am I drawn to others in need? If so, what demographic?
- What values would/do I make a point of giving to my child because I didn't have them through some lack in my childhood?

## Divine Purpose

- What is my top feminine superpower that I identify with most?

The next thing to do is to sit with these questions and their answers for a while. Maybe over several days. Spend time connecting with nature, and notice anything that comes up in your world that relates to your thoughts on this through conversations or something you catch on TV or in passing or even advertising. Something in your world will begin to trigger your thoughts on this and help you formulate it. Pay attention to your dreams too. For sure, divine purpose comes out of something we feel a deep connection with from a place of passion.

My journey in becoming an empowerer took many twists before I finally got it. I had to go through the valley of experiencing the direct opposite, oppression, to fully understand it. This was painful but sadly necessary. The defining moment for me came out of a place of pain. A realisation that I had always desired to help others but got it so wrong in my application. I felt the call, but it wasn't formulated. So instead of being empowering, I was dictatorial, judgemental, and bossy. A rescuer of people. Realisation came only when someone brought this to my attention in a confrontation. It resulted in me feeling my entire upbringing and personality were all wrong. It felt like I had the carpet of my life pulled out from under me in fact. That was the moment when I started to look at my life from the inside out. I had to find out what it was in me, that was so urgent and yet so pathetically ineffective. For six months I did not speak outside of the house to anyone unless they asked a direct question. I wanted to see what my life was without me in it. I literally took myself out to pasture.

## Rachel White

Your journey will be different. But it will have included hardships along the way which are all directing your feet into your divine purpose. I guarantee it. I know that the universe prepares our hearts through everything we experience in our lives. We get to a place where we are surrendered and able to receive.

Once we begin to align our thoughts, the universe will send answers. All we need do is be mindful to recognise it when it comes. Let's remember it is the universe that designs and decides what our divine purpose should be and is. The universe chooses; we consent and align. We will be simultaneously drawn towards it. Which is why on reviewing our lives, we can think back to some pivotal moments that enquire of the universe, What is this teaching or showing me? Is there a common theme? That's often a good indicator. Divine purpose is not about what we "fancy". It would be very dangerous to our souls to think of it this way. It is, of course, the other way around. We cannot dictate that the universe be or act or operate in a certain way. We become surrendered to it. We have to move our hearts to line up with the universe's purposes for us. We cannot impose our will. The second we try it, we will be in trouble spiritually because we will have stepped out of pure love and into control. The universe cannot be and is never under control; it is wild and free. I know I speak to your heart, my sister, because your heart wants and needs release into the wildness and freedom of the feminine.

It is very much a partnership. The universe has been calling, cooing, training, providing instances all along that are communications to our hearts. When we review our lives in the light of this, we begin to see how the universe reveals our divine purpose through our surrender, our seeking. Divine purpose unfolds.

## Divine Purpose

Find a way to petition the universe. Some like the idea of prayer. Others maybe to write a sealed note, or to ask a trusted friend as a soundboard. Please do use our *Divine Purpose* page to ask any question you wish in relation to this. Allow your sisterhood to input their goodness and wisdom into the mix too. We don't have to get clear on this in five minutes flat. I mean, we might, and if so, great. Let it evolve and gestate in your spirit. Birth it, own it, recognise what is being communicated into your heart at its innermost sacred core. This is our journey as a sisterhood and your personal journey as a woman.

I promise you will get clarity. It will come. Then you need to own it as your own because it is your own, giving thanks to the universe in your own way for it.

Fabulous. It's likely that as soon as you begin to acknowledge your divine purpose, the universe confirms it with you. My realisation and declaration of being an empowerer were both confirmed and tested within a minute. I'm not even joking; it was that fast. It may not be that way with you, but for me, the universe seems to like this method as it's happened numerous times in various contexts. I get tested on what the universe is speaking to my heart incredibly fast, and it always makes me chuckle when it happens.

On this journey into divine purpose, we never really arrive. So on that basis, we have to take our ideas out of our mindset of this being an outcome or achievement. The whole idea is that our divine purpose is a way of *being*, a fulfilment of the universe's plan to bring fulfilment to our existence. It is, in effect, a way in which we can be spiritual in a practical way. It is fluid; it is a becoming, an awakening into the deeper you. This is amazing! When we understand, it means the pressure is off. There are no targets to achieve, just a continual momentum forward. No one, not even you, can ever accuse you of being a failure in it either. Isn't that fabulous?

One of my favourite personal quotations, which is all mine, is this: "Ditch perfectionism. Go for authenticity instead." This is exactly the heart of the woman walking forward in her Divine Purpose. We forget sometimes. We do the opposite sometimes. We won't be perfect. That's okay. Just get to your feet and go again, soldier. As long as you're moving forward in the flow of your Divine Purpose, you'll be doing just great.

Your divine purpose is waiting for you at any age, so please never feel that you are the wrong age. You're not. Remember, the universe has sent you to be here in this human existence for exactly the time it is now. That's no mistake. Just move forward with this wherever you are and whatever age you may be. The ideal age to start exploring your divine purpose is in your twenties. I recommend maidens younger than seventeen wait until that age before approaching this as I believe you need to grow into yourself a little as an adult before making a commitment to this.

Our Divine Purpose is a sacred gift to us from the universe to fulfil our lives and benefit the world around us. How cool Is that? Therefore, we need to take our commitment to understanding it and applying it in our lives very seriously. It is a powerful gift and a powerful force, and not to be taken lightly. In fact, the more seriously we take it, the more committed we are to it, the more powerful it becomes.

Let's detail out a little more of how we can do this. Once we know for ourselves, we are automatically going to begin aligning with our divine purpose. Our heads (our reasoning), our hearts (our connections to pure love), and

## Divine Purpose

our guts (the inner feeling that we are on the right path) all line up.

We are ready to begin strengthening our beautiful, wonderful, awesome, unique divine purpose.

Practically, the strengthening comes quite naturally as we move forward with some finer details. The first thing to remember is that, as we said before, divine purpose sits over the entirety of our lives. So for me, wherever I go, whatever I do at work, as a mum, even when I'm shopping, wherever I am, whomever I interact with, I am an empowerer first and foremost.

We will find that we live out of our commitment to our divine purpose. The more we explore it, the deeper we go. Our hearts become all about our divine purpose. Your divine purpose is your number-one priority and naturally exudes from your pure heart. Our divine purpose becomes a framework that everything else fits into. Remember this because on a soul level, it is our calling from the universe. It is who we are at our authentic cores. How we were designed to *be*. Of course, it is going to pour out of us and through us. It's embedded deep within us, and as women, this is the essence of us rising. Think of it like a river. We are constantly in it, allowing it to pour over us. We have moved past being at the edge, dipping our toes in as we please and choose. Divine purpose, once we are awakened to it, requires us to be fully immersive, wet with it, all the time. This is why it can't be taken lightly. It's not for messing with; its power is too great. I know our hearts get this.

As a framework, divine purpose helps us choose what is best for our lives. Say, for example, your divine purpose is to be a truth teller. Everything you do has to be in the context of that. It is incongruous (not appropriate before the universe) to hold a job or career that uses deceptive tactics

## Rachel White

to get ahead, for example. Or to lie on a form, or to your mother or your kids, and so on. As a truth teller, the truth in all its facets is of the highest order. There is no room for lying, bending of the truth, or deception. Or having anyone lie to you. Everything that comes your direction is about pure truth, truth, truth. In every context you can think of. You'll also be one who exposes secrets in order to bring healing and freedom. Develop, explore, connect, expect it of others as that's how they'll grow too. Turn up that truth dial to the max. Or maybe you've been chosen to birth things, bring new ideas, perceptions, solutions into the world. That would make you a midwife of the soul. All to bring freedom, ease, and relief from suffering, an answer to someone's deep questioning. Your contribution leads them to have and own a new experience, restored, freer of oppression. Wherever you are, whatever you do, and in all situations you are your divine purpose. It is a constant flow, a oneness with the universe for the greater good. Wow, awesome.

The idea in walking forward in divine purpose is that we make mindful decisions that intentionally support its growth, development, and expansions in our lives. Can you see how your divine purpose comes right out of the feminine superpowers. Our superpowers power us up into our divine purpose. This is why I presented them to our hearts first. Our divine purpose is so important, so special we need to be really grounded within it. Consider this. If I was to have a kite—a really big, powerful one with four strings—and flying it in strong wind. Then I said, "Here, take over for a bit." If you weren't used to it or expecting it to be as strong as it was, that kite has the potential to knock you off your feet and take you by surprise. It is the same with divine purpose. It is essential to be grounded in it, to really think it through, to understand what it means for you, how it wants

## Divine Purpose

to manifest itself through your life. It's going to take some deep sessions in meditation and journaling. Our hearts, one with the universe, need to get clear on the how, what, why of the message the universe is calling us forward in. It is a heart response, a process that we can engage in. The way to walk forward is with baby steps full of tenacity, safe in the knowledge and understanding that the universe of pure love holds us in place. There is going to be a time very soon when this process is going to get us howling on the floor, releasing some things and birthing others through tears. This is all part of it, sister. Welcome those moments.

Whatever your divine purpose is, work with it, explore every facet of it, become obsessed; it's perfectly okay. Every which way you can, embrace it fully and journal about it. Pursue it like a lover. It is, in a sense, a lover of your soul. It is very definitely a way of interacting with the universe on a love basis in a practical way. Turn up the heat, sister. This is the place where we can never be accused of being "too much". Well, they can try, but it's the universe that has sent you to be. So their complaint is not really against you. Our hearts can be held safe in the assurance that no one can throw us off the track of our divine purpose. No one. If anyone ever tells you that you, in your divine purpose, are too much, let them. Let your heart know that this is exactly the place it needs to be. They are right! Except that it can never actually be *too* much. Take that as an affirmation and a confirmation that the universe is literally outworking its divine purpose in you. I almost invite that comment into my life because it is right for me to be known as an empowerer. That is who I am in my truth, so to be recognised for it is highly honourable.

Ideally, working on our divine purpose in our twenties is fabulous because we can establish the building blocks of life choices around it. That's exactly how it should be. Divine purpose comes first, and everything else fits into it, helping us define our footsteps through every decision, large and small. With it, we will not go wrong because it is not wishy-washy supposition from the universe but life-affirming, decisive, and tailored for us as individuals. No matter if we are older and more established. The journey is different, and we may have to get to a place where we review our lives in context of it. All of that is okay as long as we continue to walk forwards.

Once you are clear on your divine purpose, it is very important to choose a life partner who will support its growth in us. Ideally, choose a man (if a man is your choice) who is working on his own divine purpose. Having a heart-connected relationship with a partner of your choice means that we can talk through these very deep things without fear of rejection and ridicule. If you are with someone and feel he or she wouldn't be able to engage in this kind of conversation, you could fairly well say that this isn't the person for you. In a relationship of equal measure, both are working with and investing in each other's divine purpose. This is a power relationship that becomes all about team divine purpose, even if it's not the same divine purpose. It doesn't matter. It is the investment into each other's heart and soul, and the commitment to do so, that is so important.

Many of us struggle with the deep need of being affirmed as females on this fabulous journey of the heart. This is why being in a sisterhood is so important. That is the place where each and every feminine heart is always heard and affirmed.

For some of us more established in our lives, the journey is different. We may need to review our relationships, careers, and involvement in all sorts of things in the light of our

## Divine Purpose

divine purpose. For some, that will mean making changes. Or placing very big boundaries around relationships. With our adult children or our extended family members, for example.

Everything we can do to enhance our divine purpose we should pursue. If it is incorporated into our day job, so much the better. For example, if your divine purpose is to be a justice bringer and that's your paid employment in some form. Maybe a law enforcement role; once you come home, you are still a justice bringer. It can't be shed at the door with taking off your shoes. Your children need to see you being a justice bringer inside the home in an appropriate context. That is the beauty. Our divine purpose is always working itself out, flowing in and out of our lives. It may look different in different circumstances and contexts, but it is always there inside our life.

Our divine purpose is essentially us at the soul level. There is never a time when we put it down or away for ten minutes. The commitment it requires from us is high, but it is not and should never be a hardship. It is nothing but a joy. The universe has chosen to express its sacred self through us in this way. What an absolute honour and privilege. When we come into full awareness and awakening of this truth, it truly is humbling.

Your divine purpose is always with you. It holds steady. Even if you have to let relationships of whatever type go, or careers or maybe even the function of your body. Your divine purpose is you and will be *you* until your last breath. It is always there, guiding your path. This is absolutely brilliant news because once you know and own it, in the light of difficulties that certainly will come to your life, you can be sure that your divine purpose and the foundation that you have made it inside your life remains strong and solid. Forever.

## Rachel White

Although exciting, this is not an easy journey. There will be times when we feel wobbly, or we perhaps don't live out our divine purposes. Or our divine purpose simply may clash with other people's ways of doing things. For me, the journey of being an empowerer has been tough. I'll share with you one story.

Back in the summer of 2018, I was caring for an elderly woman with Alzheimer's. On a Tuesday, part of my duties was to go with her to a singing club. At the time, she was having some bowel trouble and feared leaving the house because of it. I was pretty certain she would be fine this particular day, and because I am an empowerer, I encouraged her and told her we should still attend. She had not been ill that day, and I wanted her to live life to the fullest. So we went along. She offered information about it to one of the workers there. Usually I have to leave before the end of the session, and the woman is transported home by the special bus. So the worker approached me and basically reprimanded me for potentially leaving them with someone who may be unwell. (She had talked about her problem with everyone there.) But I know as an empowerer, if I didn't motivate her to do things, she may never leave the house again because of the grip of fear over this issue. So you see what was going on there? My call to be an empowerer will not let me engage with the fear that others so readily display. But it for sure clashed head-on. It was not easy in the moment. I was annoyed by it. But it comes back to my being an empowerer first of all, no matter what. In every situation, every context I can think of. The woman was fine, of course; there was no issue. The universe had and always has my back. I'm convinced of that.

Expect opposition of your divine purpose. This is both a test and a confirmation that your heart is aligned. It is all good in the end. Come share your stories and tricky moments

## Divine Purpose

with the sisterhood. This is what we are all about. We simply must rise in this together, and we must help our sisters.

Your divine purpose is *your* divine purpose. It is very special and unique to you. In big ways and in small ways, when you step into and own it, your divine purpose has the power to change the world. So go for it, sister. Go for it!

# CHAPTER 8

# *The Wounded Feminine*

> It is easy for people to joke about scars if they have never been cut.
> —William Shakespeare, 1564–1616

Our feminine, beautiful, glorious hearts have been damaged in numerous ways through the centuries. It's an appalling travesty and tragedy that affects each of our lives from every angle. Through the ricochet of time and the legacy passed down through each generation of mother to daughter, and through to our continued experiences that creep in daily, in big and small ways. All of this contributes to the wounded feminine. There is so much here we could talk about that merits a book all its own. But in this chapter, I home in on some key aspects that are common to all our experiences.

## Divine Purpose

Living this life, having a human experience as a female being, is not an easy road. My intention here is that together, we will be able to look at some of these wounds in a general sense, identify them, and bring them out to the surface, into the light, so that we can begin to get clarity and healing. This whole chapter will be a trigger for some of us. But I would like us to really embrace what's coming up here in our hearts and face it. It may well be that some of us need some extra support through counselling and therapy. This is all good. I urge you to seek that out if you feel you need it because now is your time. It has to be in order to do what we are called to do through our divine purpose and to stand in our rising power, hand in hand with our gathered sisters. We need to be healthy, whole, and restored. Our hearts long to break out of the ropes that have bound them in pain for so long. We cannot fully enter into divine purpose if we keep hurt, pain, and fear alive in our hearts. See, those things are bigger and more real to us in our lives than the love of the universe that sent us. That's the wrong way round, so we need to do something about it.

It's imperative we address the wounds of the feminine as part of this journey. You see, we need a risen sisterhood, strong and standing together, walking forward each in one's divine purpose. The wounds have come to squash us and keep us small and ineffective. We know now that we need to be in a place where we do the opposite. We need to grow big in our spirits, and we need to rise. We can't rise into our fullness if we are bound by the chains of that which wounds us. Can you see what I'm saying?

We want and need things to change so desperately for our beautiful daughters, the maidens of the next generation. No way do we want them to experience some of the struggles and outright abuses we've had to face. There has to be a change, and it's up to us to promote and facilitate it. To generate enough heartfelt groundswell so that there is no option. The intolerance against feminine power in all its glorious fullness needs to come to an end. It is long beyond time.

So for ourselves and for the generations of women to come, let's deal with our wounded feminine. If we unpack it to see what is really going on, we will find it is actually a deep wound to our vulnerability.

How we operate rightly as feminine beings is partly due to our wonderful vulnerability. That's part of our feminine essence. It is and *should be* part of who we are at our core. Our common experience is that we have taken all that precious vulnerability out of ourselves, laid it bare, put it openly on the table before others, and taken the risk only to have this wounding come in and smash it—us—with a hammer. That is what it feels like. We are supposed to be vulnerable; the feminine is designed by the universe to be vulnerable. It is how we give our all and how we invest in emotions, relationships, and energy exchanges of all kinds to find our true place in the soul, where we can sit as the queen in our lives. However, the problem is that as soon as we express this vulnerability, it opens the door for this wounding to come in.

The result of this battering is that we shut our hearts down, we turn our vulnerability to stone, and we lose our softness. Once we lose our softness, we compromise our feminine essence. We, understandably, contribute to the squashing of the feminine. Dear sister, I know these words are hard to hear. Please understand my heart. My intention is not to add to the blame and judgement but to explain the process of how this occurs. We are caught in a pernicious loop, a trap which is not our fault. In order to rise, we need

## Divine Purpose

to recognise this and turn it around. We must rise into our divine purpose. This means that anything that holds us back, constrained, or kept small must be resolved in our hearts so that we can move forward in the fullness of our own power.

For sure many of us have known the deep wounding that comes when our bodies have been violated. This is a serious wounding of the feminine. But deep wounding can come even if we have not had our bodies violated. Our beautiful feminine essence is our vulnerability. It is that which becomes squashed and repressed inside us. When those deep wounds come into our feminine core, our inner she, it is as though we have taken out the precious gifts of our very selves and been told again and again and again that we are not enough. Not clever enough, pretty enough, talented enough, thin enough. On and on with this not "being enough-ness". Sometimes this is said without words. For the beautiful maiden who has been beaten, raped, abused, the unspoken message has been, "Not good enough to be given respect." For the one who has been bullied, "Not good enough to be acceptable." Many of us have known the sting of rejection in our ears as we heard those actual words. This dreadful message of not enough comes in millions of ways to our souls. My ears have heard obscenities screamed at me too. Well, let's agree right here and right now that we, you and I, are enough. We are enough! More than enough. You see, before this wound came into our souls, there was a deeper agreement between the universe of pure love and light and life and ourselves on a heart and soul level. The universe that sent us into being, that breathed life into our very hearts, that universe of pure love sent you and I each with a divine purpose to fulfil. That original agreement still stands. It is bigger, greater, deeper, fuller than any abuser or incoming wound tried to make with our hearts as some sort of soul contract without our consent. We break that agreement of the wound by aligning with the universe that sent us in the first place. The acknowledgement of our original agreement with that energy of love from the universe changes our hearts forever. Refuse to continue to concede to the energy of fear, hate, revenge, and other negative emotions that the wounding brought into our lives. We no longer partner or agree with it because it does not give life to our souls. It does not promote love. Therefore, it is not in alignment with the universe and has no place in our hearts. Women of destiny, my sisters, we rise!

> Let it be so.
>
> *Author's Note:* Take a little time to journal and process these things that we have shared here. Give your heart room, time, and space to be heard and held.

Earlier in this book, we said that comparison and competition are expressions of masculine energy. We have been sold these ideas as we've been made to fit into a male nine-to-five construct of a world. The result has been that in order to fit and feel accepted, we felt we needed to be just like men in order to be taken seriously by them. In our pursuit of needing to be acknowledged and our misunderstanding of what is going on at a spiritual level in our inner she, we've become pseudo-males. Some of us more than others. All of this produces the outcome of the feminine essence being squashed down and out of us in the subconscious belief that the feminine, at best, is secondary and at worst, just never enough and is wrong somehow.

My darlings, we need to look seriously at this in our lives.

## Divine Purpose

Without realising it and by trying to secure equality and fairness with men, we have taken them on at their own game. This has led us unwittingly up the garden path of agreeing with patriarchy instead of realising and standing in our own power. This has also caused a deep feminine wound. In my observations, males show confusion in their own hearts about the true feminine. Our misunderstandings, our hurt have been great, along with our inability to communicate effectively into the hearts of men to ensure they understand. No wonder, if we have been lax and fearful in showing them our authentic hearts. That is not our fault. Not at all. Patriarchy rears its ugly head around every corner. However, we have the power, by coming into our true feminine, to challenge the ingrained beliefs of males and smash centuries' worth of assumed dominance if we come together and stand in our true feminine power. We have the power. I totally believe it.

There is so much to say about the wounded feminine. More than this chapter will allow. However, I have one more important point to make. That is, as a sisterhood, let us never be found wounding each other. Sure, we may mess up. But let us hold space and be quick to allow each other right back into the fold and shelter of each other's arms and hearts. Be quick to offer peace to each other in a sisterhood, the company of women, the place that I'm describing like a golden thread through this book. When I talk about the "gathered sisterhood", I mean we simply must stand together as one with clean hearts. No resentments, no grudges, no hang ups, between any of our hearts. The worst thing a woman can do to a sister, even if she is not known, is to be intimate with another sister's partner. (That is the ultimate betrayal of her, your sister). Please, for your sisters' sakes, never get intimately involved in that kind of thing. It will damage all our hearts. It completely breaks down the premise of rising together if we introduce oppression, which means to stand against. We need to do absolutely everything we can to prevent the wounded feminine from going any further. Let's stop it in its tracks at all levels. Freedom, sisters! Do you hear the call? May your heart sing a song of freedom from the deep wounds of the feminine.

Clarity is coming to our hearts, and we can see our paths a little more clearly. In order to rise in our feminine, our power and glory. I know you feel your heart shifting to a new place, where you no longer feel that the wounds and hurts of old should own or have any power over you. That's absolutely right. Sweetheart, you belong to you. Right before and inside of the universe, our life force. The pain does not own or hold you. You are a precious pearl. No longer shall you cast your heart and gifts before swine. The twin demons of negativity and resentment shall not have our hearts. Reclaim and rise, dear sister. Reclaim and rise.

# CHAPTER 9

# *The Inner She and the Outer She*

> I was grounded while you filled the skies
> I was dumbfounded by truth you cut through lies
> I saw the rain dirty valley, you saw Brigadoon
> I saw the crescent you saw the whole of the moon.
>
> —"The Whole of the Moon," Michael Scott/The Waterboys

This amazing duality of how we are as feminine beings is incredible. I use these terms the "inner she" and the "outer she" all of the time, so I feel it's helpful for us to know what I'm talking about. It's my own description of what the universe has revealed to me about how the feminine essence truly operates. Once we understand how the inner and outer she work, everything we've previously talked about in this book slides into place in our hearts.

## Rachel White

The outer she is the part of us we choose to present to the world. It includes the body, the way we choose to clothe it, mannerisms and body language, the way we walk, if we choose to wear make-up or not, how we have our hair, our words, our voice. The outer she is everything we choose to present to the world externally that gives others information about who we are. As the part of us others can see and access, this is the part of us that is open to judgement by others about what the feminine, or our expression of femininity, is. Who decides that anyway? In our own way, we too have fallen into that same trap, though we now know that true femininity resides in the heart. Our perceptions have changed; I hope that we know that, having journeyed through this book so far together. Truly if we are clear and secure that our hearts are in alignment with our life force, it should not and does not matter in a spiritual way what we physically show up as. It is all about the heart. At the same time, however, we have to be mindful that the way in which others have access to our inner she, to get to really know the heart of us is through the outer she.

The outer she is important because this is where we demonstrate and express what is in our hearts. So how we appear to the external world needs to come from a place of our understanding that we have the power to invite people into our goodness and our purity of spirit, which to a point of our choosing, we are willing to share with them. It is their access point, a way in to get to know the true, authentic us. The invitation is not open season for judgement from their hearts or even from our own. This is why our inner she needs to be very strong. Being soft and open through our outer she gives out the message that we are the most sacred, awesome, beautiful beings on the planet. We come to a place where we realise that the outer she is intentionally soft. In comparison

## Divine Purpose

to a male body, our bodies are soft so that we can be nurturers and comforters. If we think about the sexual act between a man and woman, the man is hard, and the woman is soft. This is the design of the Universe. We literally welcome a man into our soft bodies, our curves, our touch, so that he may receive that softness. He cannot access softness any other way—not really—because it doesn't reside in him in the way it does with us. It is an amazing observation that a man in the arms of the woman he adores surrenders his hard exterior in the afterglow of his orgasm. It is as though in her glorious presence, he becomes malleable. Without threat, he embraces some of her softness for himself. He lays down the internal warrior that seems to be on guard and fighting within his own masculine all the time. The inner boy is called forth from the man (although not for long) in a spiritual context, whether he is aware of it or not. A man desires to make love to a woman, to penetrate her, in order to access her heart. It is our vulnerability, our softness, and our comfort he so requires. This is the truth, although no man would ever put it that way when his penis is ready for action. This is the basis of the sexual act becoming sacred.

Of course, we are soft too in nourishing and cuddling our newborns. Breastfeeding is a fantastic expression of nurture, comfort, sustenance, softness, and connection rolled into one. Our bodies are designed for this. Not just functionally but emotionally and spiritually also.

So we see that the outer she is very important. I am of the opinion that anything we can do to enhance and accentuate that feeling of softness expressed in our outer she in the fabrics we choose to wear or the way we move our bodies or use our voices can draw people into our realm. It is invitational. People feel safe with us, maybe trusted. It is very engaging. Our souls become attractive, and people begin to understand us better simply because we are more mindfully aware that our feminine essence is awakening. It is all part of rising into our female power. If we are looking to attract a life partner to even begin to look in our direction, treating our outer she, well, in this mindset, is a great place to start. Clothes, shoes, hair, make-up, body language, attitude, verbal responses. With all these things, think soft, soft, soft in order extend, dwell on, and promote our feminine essence. Softness, or the unspoken feeling of it, is essential to the world and to ourselves at the same time. Our outer she feeds our internal world, our inner she, in a continual feedback loop to reaffirm our hearts in our feminine essence. It is all about our hearts first. What other yardsticks people choose to judge us by is their business. Nothing to do with us.

The inner she is a whole different place that is not on view to the world but is certainly known to us. It is our internal place that no one sees, but it is expressed through the outer she when we allow our vulnerabilities to shine through.

The inner she is where we are strong and resolute. The inner she holds one's

- Self-identity
- Sense of the sacred
- Values and honour of others
- Boundaries
- Divine purpose

Once we are clear, really clear, and resolved in these areas and working on our continued alignment within the universe, something amazing happens. We become unshakeable! Nothing and no one can get us off track. By

## Divine Purpose

that I mean we cannot be detracted, derailed, or distracted from our precious alignment with the universe. We are held safe and secure.

So what we are saying here is that we get aligned with the universe through our inner she. Our heart connections, our energy to relate always come from that place of the inside first and through to the outside, the outer she.

Interestingly, the masculine energy in males operates in the opposite way. They feel and connect through their hard exterior to reach the soft place inside. The feminine essence is soft on the outside, hard on the inside; the masculine is hard on the outside and soft on the inside.

The inner she is where we truly reside. The real us, the real you, the real me. Some may term this the "divine feminine". It is our inner core, our heart, our soul. This is who we truly are. It is the part of us that connects deeply with the universe and makes deep connections, heart connections, with others we recognise are on similar heart journeys to ourselves.

The inner she and the outer she work in unison, constantly flowing beautifully together, weaving in and out. This is what gives the feminine essence a sense of holiness, the sacred embodiment of the true feminine. When we recognise this, we can see and experience the depth, majesty, and power of what it is to be and embrace true femininity within ourselves and recognise it in our sisters too.

With our outer she, we are able to influence and guide our inner she, whilst the inner she directs our choices for the outer she. We are able to intentionally place our own footsteps and work out practical applications of how we think, feel, and respond in our outer she directed by the solidity, the assurance that we hold in our inner she.

This is always at work whether we recognise it or not.

This is why when we have a wound of the feminine coming through the outer she, it embeds itself in our feminine core, our inner she. What if that which is a thing of hurt and pain is held in the inner she and is ignored, left unacknowledged? We have fed her with a negative emotion and held it there. Then, when it is time for us to respond (maybe when that wound is poked with a hot rod, a fancy way to describe being triggered), we find that what we have held in our inner she is the resource we draw from with our outer she and have nothing to offer in return, except the product of that hurt and pain. This is one reason it is so important to know your inner she so very well. The effect held energy can have on yourself and others, and how that same negative energy can affect you if it is inbound from others, is very real. Of course, the reverse is more than true. It is this that we seek to promote within ourselves. That is why empowerment, nourishment, and restoration of the soul are such healing balms. (See how our feminine superpowers fit into this?) Energy always resonates and has an impact at the heart and soul level. Even if we choose to ignore it, it still exists; it still vibrates in our soul as a ripple effect.

Unresolved, held wounds in the inner she can manifest in physical symptoms of illness and diseases affecting mind and body. We've all realised for some time now that this really is how our bodies operate when in distress. Here together, we've unpacked a little of how the outer and inner she flow together to produce this effect.

My call to us as women of destiny on a heart journey is that we understand this process and do and be everything we can to enhance the flow of positive energy flow within ourselves. This is our real healing and restoration. The real work of raising our feminine.

A very large part of us rising into the true, powerful

## Divine Purpose

feminine essence is about solidifying the inner she, the place where we do not compromise ourselves and where truth abounds. Our truth floods our soul. Let's look at some of those areas we listed previously. This is something to spend time journaling out and meditating about what it is that brings these things up for you in your spirit.

*Self-Identity:* Do we truly know who we are? Do we know our power, who we are in spirit? Do we know we are sent and loved and held by the universe for no other reason than just being us? At this point, it is so worthwhile to head back to our first chapter. Because our hearts have been on a journey of awakening as we've read through this book so far and worked on various aspects, rereading the first chapter will bring new questions and fresh insights. Recognise that this is the process. You are definitely growing in spirit, rising. You are getting more and more beautiful, sister, from within. Go ahead; take the time you need to be with yourself as you let these thoughts wash over you and permeate your soul. There is no rush.

*The Sacred:* The sense of the sacred is beyond incredible, the measure of our natural understanding. Our connection to the universe is exceptionally special and is to be treasured, honoured, and respected above all else. Our alignment is a spiritual umbilical cord. Damage caused by disrespect of it results in losing the lifeblood to our source. This means we will die, spiritually speaking. Actually, we will be worse than dead. We would be spiritual zombies, open to all manner of evil.

The sacred is so precious; it is a gift. It is also a communion, a common union with that life force power. Through our heart connection we receive all that is good from the source of love, light, and life. At the same time, the life force raises us to be conduits of its expression of love, light, and life. It is a two-way street, exactly like the umbilical cord. No wonder because that is the pattern it was designed from. We dare not treat this lightly.

Of course, because as we connect with sacred, the sacred also becomes alive in us, and we become sacred. Our reality then becomes more about the purposes of the desires of the universe (always to bring life through love) than it is about us achieving our own agenda of selfish ambition through ego. The sense of the sacred becomes stronger and stronger in us the more we travel this path. It is of great importance that we take time to honour the sacred within us every day. It is the seat of respectfulness for all things. We are evolving to embed that within our inner she. Once we have it, when we encounter disrespect and that sense of "casting our pearls before swine", we will recognise it instantly within our inner she. We will have the strength and power to be solid in our stance against it. All that is precious, especially the feminine essence, will not be trashed. Not because we are staunch feminists, even if we are, but because we hold the sacred feminine within; we become the sacred feminine. It is embedded within, and we are the embodiment of it. Yes, that cannot be trashed!

To get to the place of understanding the sacred, we must love ourselves unconditionally for all that we are. Every emotion and feeling that arises within us needs to be acknowledged. If we can give thanks, seeing every emotion as perfectly valid, we cease to serve ego. We begin to love ourselves authentically. Our sacred comes through our complete acceptance of ourselves.

*Our Values and Our Honour of Others:* Within our inner she, we have an amazing capacity to help and hold others. We are fully able to give, give, give. To date, I have met no woman without the ability to give too much in every

## Divine Purpose

way imaginable. The flip side of this is that we tend to denigrate men, in general, for being selfish. But I question if that's the case with most. Or are we framing them in the light of our self-defined selflessness. That needs exploration because, of course, a man is going to look and feel "selfish" to us standing next to our yardstick of selfishness. Or are we jealous that he is able, because of his conditioning, to be that way? Oh, such beautiful heart work to be done here.

What is your truth, sister, in your heart? This issue creates many feelings of imbalance in too many relationships, causing damage because we have misaligned our value of ourselves. We've never had much permission or opportunity to really think through how we really feel, how we are on this, how we value ourselves. As young girls, we're given the message time and time and time again that to think of our needs, wants, choices, preferences, and opinions is selfish. The little girl is seen somehow as inherently selfish for even daring to think of herself, let alone voice it. Even the Brownie Guide/Scout motto for seven-year-old girls is, "To think of others before yourself." The problem is that if we are taught this and always do this, we never think of ourselves. Unless we are girls who grew up in a box, there is always someone else to think about first. Seven-year-old girls quote this statement to each other every week as we did if we attended those meetings. The church also teaches us to deny ourselves. Again, in the mind of the blossoming female heart, this sends the direct message that somehow we are deliberately, wilfully selfish, made that way, and need to be reined in. Let me say here and now, it's lies, and we need to resolve it.

As girls growing up, we were handed emotional situations and embraced our emotional lives not being helped much to see that we had a choice of response or reaction. Blamed, criticised, rejected when our emotions, valid and necessary parts of our female essence, came racing to the surface of our psyche.

What is it that is in our value systems? Do we honour ourselves highly or succumb to damping down? How often do we put ourselves and our needs first, above others? Why? How does that make us feel? These are very real questions to explore and will give us insight into the state of our hearts.

Our word is our bond, so a healthy exercise is to catch ourselves in the act of talking about ourselves. Are we letting our physical ears hear things from our lips that build up our inner she? Are we kind to ourselves? Are we truthful with and about ourselves in front of others, to our own hearts? Or do we do that false humility thing of not accepting compliments or disagreeing if someone endorses us?

How do we regard others? Are beloved friends and family different from strangers in this regard? Do we hold people in different spaces in our hearts depending on our relationships with them? Should we? These are huge questions that we can spend time grappling with. I believe it is worth it. I'm going to say something else quite profound: You are the most important person in your life. No one is with you, as committed to your heart journey, and as present in your life as much as you are. This means that we must do the work of feeding our souls good food. We cannot depend on others even 1 per cent to pick up the tab of that responsibility.

Our values are literally something of great worth, a precious, expensive possession. You are the prize, the apple of your own eye, the precious jewel. We have everything that the universe has given us—all our feminine superpowers, our softness, our heart connections, our gifts and talents, our divine purpose. Every resource of the creative life force. This is you and I, dearest sister. Out of recognising and claiming

## Divine Purpose

our own values, we firstly teach others how to value us as a pearl of great price. Immensely valuable. Secondly, we will automatically know how to value others. It comes very easily once we understand ourselves better that people, their hearts, and their souls are exceptionally precious. We begin to want the best for them in every context, and we treat them accordingly.

For some of us, we have constant encounters with toxic people, the soul killers in our lives. We all know what we mean by that. Those who suck the energy right out of the room with their presence. Everything coming from them is about the negative. For sure if they are abusive, they are a soul killer. Without doubt, they are extremely hurt, very damaged in their inner core. There are times when it is right to help them to see our light. However, I have come to the very sad conclusion, through my experience, that it is far better to remove our precious selves from their presence and influence. If they are adults, we cannot save them from themselves. That is never our job. But we can hand the responsibility back to them. We cannot get them aligned with light and life. Only they can do that in their responses to the universe on their terms. We need to recognise that we may have to walk away for our own sake. If we do, we can be confident in knowing that it is still a case of us very much valuing and honouring them. Not the abandonment and rejection they may accuse us of. Walking away, cutting ties is often the most empowering thing we can ever do for them. One last sacred gift from our precious heart.

What are your values, sister? Are you your top priority? Getting our heads and hearts around this is foundational in making our inner she strong, strong, strong.

*Boundaries:* Oh, my. At the beginning of this book, when we talked about this being for strong hearts, I was talking to my own heart. You see, I am weak in this area. I have struggled, and I need help big time. So I'm writing this section for myself as a permanent record, so I can look back and access what my inner she wants to teach me. If you also find this helpful, I hope you will join with my heart on this wild ride.

Boundaries make us very strong. Never has there been such a need for the feminine heart to safeguard itself with some strong boundaries. Boundaries are literally fences. I feel in my life, in my youth, I was misdirected to understand that boundaries are walls around our hearts. The instruction coming at me was that these should always be smashed down in order to make us open and soft-hearted. I now realise my truth on this is entirely different, which is why I've written this entire book. The boundary fence is there to keep us safe and the wolf out. Not to build a prison camp for our hearts. Traditionally and historically, we have been very ineffective in setting and keeping boundaries. We've been instructed to be tolerant of everyone, give to everyone else, and to make room and space for others to have their way, often at our expense. We've been railroaded into decisions, exploited, abused even. We've been under the expectation to take it all on board, as the person doing this stuff is hurting, that we might hurt their feelings, make it worse for them, damage them in some way, destroy their reputations, and so on. I know this is my journey through this. I'm quite sure that if I'm feeling it, sister, it touches on some of your experiences too. We need to get this out; it needs to be said. It's time our hearts got to the top of our priority lists.

The end product of all this is that we squash our beautiful feminine selves. Once again, the glorious feminine, our true selves are damped down, restrained, held back because of all this considering others more worthy; more important

## Divine Purpose

is that this is the antithesis of rising. Of course, under this constraint, our "squashed-ness" will not allow us to fully step into our divine purpose that the universe has sent for us. We will be more restricted than released, more crushed, and defeated. That is not our rightful, proper place. If we allow it to continue, it will kill the soul.

We need to be clear about our boundaries. What it is we will and will not tolerate from others? What will we not or no longer engage with? What are our preferences and choices? Knowing these things so intimately means that we can fully engage with our divine purpose and truth.

I had a person in my life who often called me a bitch. It was just a word, a parlance, for this person who argued that it was done in jest, done as a term of endearment. I didn't agree. However, my decision to live as an empowerer in accordance with my divine purpose and choice to walk as a queen (more on that in the next chapter) means I cannot have anyone call me that. It does nothing to empower me and detracts from my value. I made it clear that I didn't want to be called that ever again. Then it happened again. This time the person screamed at me over and over that I was a f***** bitch. That's a line crossed. My boundary line. The relationship, in my opinion, manifested such extreme toxicity. It was finished right there and then in that moment.

Our boundaries are strong, very strong. Remember in *Lord of the Rings*, where Gandalf strikes his spear in the collapsing stone stairway? He says to that demonic beast, "You shall not pass!" That is exactly what boundary setting does for us. It is exactly like that! That is its purpose; that is the attitude to adopt. "No, you shall not pass me and my boundary." In that moment, see what also happens? The Hobbits go free. Boundary setting provides safe passage and freedom for others as well as ourselves. This is one of the most empowering things we can do. The demon falls away.

What are some of your boundaries, sister? What is it you need to communicate and detail out to your heart? Make these clear to yourself; know them. Then make them known to people, not in a judgemental, accusatory way, but in a way that honours and frames what you prefer. Stand in that truth. If a person cannot hear or respect that, call that individual out on it without judgement, and then move on. Our boundaries are for us. Most people are quick to apologise and reconcile if an offense has been caused. Be very determined to recognise the boundaries of others, and be quick to sort out any offense. Become all about the high honour of boundaries. This makes us strong in our inner she.

*Our Divine Purpose:* Everything we have talked about in this book is rooted and grounded in knowing our divine purpose. Once we are clear on it, really clear, we can move forward with an absolute burning fire under our feet (in a good way). Everything comes together. Our values, our boundaries, our sense of self-identity, our sacred are all woven together into position. Divine purpose, our gift from and to the universe is taking us in a direction that wholly aligns us inside of ourselves and inside of the universe that sent and holds us . Once we know that, we know, that we know we have that solidity and security inside our inner she. It is incredible as it anchors us completely in more ways than even we realise. More than I even realise.

Remember that this is a journey, a process. Mindfully, intentionally working with the honing of our inner she, making our

- Self-identities
- Sense of the sacred

- Values
- Boundaries
- Divine purpose

strong and aligned within ourselves before the universe. It makes us very strong; we will literally be able to rise from within. It is an incredibly powerful place. Our inner she, which is manifested through our outer she, and then out into our realms, our spheres, our queendoms. We become unshakeable! Unshakeable!

## CHAPTER 10

# *Sit on Your Throne, and Wear Your Crown*

> You are so beautiful to me.
> —Billy Preston and Bruce Fisher

Each of us beautiful girls is a gorgeous queen. Do you feel gorgeous? Once we connect with our feminine selves on a deep level by expanding our inner she. I guarantee that we will. The female being is the pinnacle of all of creation. It is time for us to recognise this, reclaim our thrones, wear our crowns, and own our queendoms.

We have incredible feminine power. It doesn't, of course, look anything like masculine power Which is what we are so used to seeing. It is a misunderstanding to feel that we are in competition with men for their power. That sense of, "Got to do like them, be like them, achieve better than them to be accepted." That may be so in limited

## Divine Purpose

circumstances, but let's think about that. It's still men who have set the patriarchal terms of how women should be taken seriously and us trying to reach that ideal. No, no. That is not at all how it should be. Once we enter into competition with the masculine, we challenge male energy on its own terms. Sister, we, you and I, have our own power. It operates on the basis of cooperation and collaboration. It is entirely different and has nothing to do with the competitive and comparison energy of the masculine. We have our own throne, our own crown, our own queendom. Let's get to it because it remains empty, unworn, and weeded over unless we claim it.

Patriarchy has deceived us and squashed us from understanding that *everything* about the feminine is good.

*What kind of queen are you?* I wonder. On New Year's Day 2017, revelation kicked in for me that I was indeed a queen. Dearest sister, if I am a queen, then you also are a precious queen too. I decided that I wanted to step into my understanding of how this would play out in my life. The very first thing I did was to buy some hair accessories. You know, the Alice band styles, in different colours. I committed to wearing a different one each day as the mood dictated. It was a physical reminder to me that whenever I caught a glimpse of myself, I was stepping into my queendom by wearing a kind of crown. It was incredibly helpful for my outer she to have a constant reminder of who I am within the universe. One sent with a divine purpose. A queen.

The beautiful thing is that queenship is here for all of us. All we need do is identify it. Once we do, we are well on the way to rising into our feminine. As we totally should be.

Each queen has her own queendom. The beautiful thing is my queendom loves your queendom. We are at peace with each other; we do not fight for territory or resources. We are completely resolved in recognising our boundaries, secure in knowing what we have is all good. There is no threat because what the universe has given you is unique to you. It cannot be taken or stolen, only given in love and shared. That is how our queendoms work. Each queendom has its own flavour, its own scent of perfume with its unique values. My queendom coexists with yours and yours with mine. My heart is that your queendom will overflow with an abundance of love and health and peace. I am not threatened by your queendom, I am for the expansion of your queendom. No queen and her queendom is ever superior to another. There is no, not ever a queen amongst queens or queen of queens.

The only place that premise is not necessarily true is in the heart of a man who is totally committed to and in love with his chosen queen. Then it is right for him and him alone to regard his queen as the queen amongst queens. The same is true for a female partnership, where both queens claim each other as their queen of queens.

Our queendoms have us in their centre, sitting on our thrones, wearing our crowns, and radiating outwards. It includes within it all that we are responsible for and all that we love. In essence, what I'm describing here is the very real way our feminine presence is larger than us. It extends beyond our physical bodies. Of course, there is no limit to that expansion. Within our queendoms, we as queens ensure that our values are upheld. These are the values of your queendom. Your inner she. This is your energy. Even though it cannot be seen in the physical realm with your earthly eyes, you can feel it; it is tangible. Our queendom is the inner she and outer she working together. The parts of us that extend way beyond our experiences of ourselves have the power to inspire others. Creating a release of our

## Divine Purpose

energy as we lead by example. It is this essence of us and our divine purpose that are remembered when we leave a room, a situation, or a relationship. It is what we leave behind at the end of our lives too. Our legacy.

Put on your crown, oh, queen. You come first in your queendom. You are highly honoured. At the same time, you know how to honour the queen next to you. Wearing your crown, metaphorically speaking, is all about knowing that you belong to yourself, standing up for and being in your truth, putting yourself first.

You have a throne; a throne is a seat of power. The power to decide what you will and will not accept within your queendom, the sphere of your feminine presence. You have the ultimate right to banish all that is not within your values—hopefully based on love and light—from your presence, from your queendom.

I find it especially helpful as a mum to think of my physical space, my home environment, as my queendom. Of course, as it is a spiritual place, it is so much more than that. My understanding starts there. I have a high expectation that people who come close to my feminine presence will catch a whiff of the scent of my queendom (at the least) and will come into that place of respect for it. Of me as its queen.

Of course, our divine purpose, sent to us by the universe to fulfil, is not ever meant for us to keep to ourselves. It is world-changing power. Divine purpose, in its fullness, fuels our queendoms. The more we pursue our divine purpose and become living, breathing embodiments of it, the stronger our queendom becomes. A solid, secure, strong queen oozes her divine purpose out of every pore.

I spent some time writing out some of the values of my queendom. I hope you find them helpful, although each queen has her own. Every queendom is different, however, we weave and flow together. Here are some of my queendom's values.

- Everyone in my queendom is highly honoured and respected.
- Creativity is encouraged and affirmed.
- We will have abundance and not lack for anything.
- An empowering, permission-giving, life-affirming atmosphere will be cultivated.
- Boundaries will be strong and always well maintained.
- Other queendoms will be fully recognised, becoming cooperative partnerships.

Each queen is different with a different emphasis which fully supports your divine purpose, of course. So let's explore which type of queen we identify with within our hearts. There are three main types, although more do exist. Examining all the queen types in depth requires another book, so here I deal with the main ones.

> *Author Note:* Credit goes to Molesey Crawford, author of Unlocking the Queen Code, for these ideas. Check out her work on YouTube.

*Warrior Queens:* This amazing queen is a leader, a trailblazer. She paves the way for her sister queens to follow in the wake of her robe. She is not superior but knows how to set an example. She can almost see into the future and will give her life to the cause of promoting her sister Queens. She may be an activist or an empowerer. The war she fights within the context of her divine purpose is to bring freedom

*Divine Purpose*

and life, and to raise the feminine. We have had some incredible warrior queens.

- Emmeline Pankhurst, suffragette: Helped secure the right for women to vote … Warrior queen
- Harriet Tubman: Born a slave, she helped establish a network of safe houses known as the underground railroad so that enslaved people could escape … Warrior queen
- Katherine Switzer, runner: Entered the Boston Marathon when the rules stated it was a male-only event as women were considered "too fragile". When the organisers realised she was running, they tried to forcibly remove her from the race. Her courage and determination opened the door for other women to participate equally in sporting events … Warrior queen

These examples are just drops in the ocean. Most warrior queens are not well known, and they operate in a whole range of trailblazing contexts. But their influence and legacies have the power to live larger and longer than they ever dreamed possible.

*Messenger Queens:* These gorgeous queens come with a message and/or help others to get their voices heard. They are excellent communicators, teachers, listeners, storytellers, writers, maybe artists even. They know how to express feelings and to help others understand things that are deep within hearts. They know how to get feelings out and be heard. Messenger queens know how to draw others in and to draw out the best in terms of action, ideas, and potential from those around her. Brilliant messenger queens we may know are:

- Oprah Winfrey, broadcaster/actress/freedom activist: Developed a prime-time TV show that enabled people to share their deepest vulnerabilities and still feel safe. Became an actress to depict roles that challenged people's understanding and perceptions. Became an activist to promote freedoms for ordinary people in a variety of contexts. Is considered a voice to the nation (USA). Her influence against oppression is outstanding … Messenger queen
- Maya Angelou, author: She wrote exquisitely about her experiences growing up with the injustices that racism brought. She became both a voice of expression for all those with similar experiences and an inspiration for others to find their own voices … Messenger queen
- Catherine Corless, amateur historian. She researched and wrote letters to expose the cover-up of a mass grave in a septic tank. The bodies of 796 infants were disposed there after neglect and abuse at Ireland's Tuam Mother and Baby Home … Catherine exposed it. Messenger queen

The messenger queen uses her power of communication profoundly to change and challenge ideas surrounding injustice and oppression. She builds her queendom around getting her voice and her truth and that of others heard.

*Peace Queens:* These beautiful queens promote peace. They are all about reconciliation, restoration of relationships, and diplomacy in every way that they can imagine. Between individuals, families, and nations, they are there promoting peace. These queens largely go unnoticed, but their work is very significant and important. Here are a few world-changing queens.

*Divine Purpose*

- Miriam Coronel-Ferrer, professor of political science: She signed a final peace accord on behalf of the government of the Philippines with a rebel group to allow freedom for her people ... Peace queen
- Gabriele von Lutzau, flight attendant: Known as the "Angel of Mogadishu", she provided comfort and acted as a heroine during a plane hijack. Her actions very possibly saved the lives of many of her passengers ... Peace queen
- Yoko Ono, pacifist: She developed, amongst many other initiatives, the LennonOno Peace Award to give to people who have made a valuable contribution to the cause of peace around the world. Yoko is committed (as was her murdered husband, John Lennon) to inspiring people to adopt peace in every context ... Peace queen

I hope you'll be inspired to consider yourself as a queen. Which queen trait do you identify with the most? Wear that crown, girlfriend. The universe has given this gift to you. You are a queen.

*The Dark Queens:* We absolutely must talk about the dark queens simply because we've all been there and done that. For sure we all know women like this.

Inside our beautiful feminine hearts is a desperate longing to be *really heard, really seen, really acknowledged,* and *really validated.* That's absolutely 100 per cent how we should be. This is how the feminine operates; we are queens. But sometimes, this deep need and longing comes out of us, manifesting in a wonky way. We see it in our attention-seeking grandiosity and upstaging of others. We know when we encounter it; our inner resonance is one of *urgggh!* Or we may intuit or observe it in others without judgement. Our recognition of it is as an ugliness of spirit, a sense of harshness. This is completely understandable as we haven't been taught about how being feminine in our inner she really works. So the blossoming female heart is left to her own devices, learning to react from fear rather than respond from a place of love. Our mothers did their best to help our hearts, even though they too struggled. We know it can't be done this way, and this is why we—all of us—so desperately need our sisters gathered around us. Our traumas, our childhood experiences of how we were valued all play a part in how we view ourselves in the light of this need. Precious hearts desire and long to be handled very, very carefully. This is the heart of our sister, we know this need touches her deeply. Let us handle each other with care. Right now in our world, I sense that the feminine essence in the majority of women, especially in younger maidens, is severely wounded. It is our task, our responsibility to help them see the depths their hearts reach. One of the problems has been that in our drama queen moments, there's a fragile point when the inner she received the message about being too much or not enough. The last thing we want to do is add to that.

Let's help all of us who have been a drama queen—and that's all of us—to see this clearly and help each other rise into full queenship.

The drama queen who lives in her drama most of her time feels this need very strongly. In her underdeveloped heart, she is expressing a need to be really seen, really heard, and really acknowledged. This need is so strong, in her insecurity, she demands it be met by others through her attention-seeking behaviour, getting them to notice her and respond. She has not yet learned that by just being

## Divine Purpose

and owning her queenship, she will gain the very thing she desires.

Paradoxically, the need in her is so strong, she pushes forward in strife, demand, and strops. These actions bring her the opposite. So in her immature nature, she pushes harder, until the day she rises from this disillusionment through the realisation that this doesn't work and doesn't bring the fulfilment she desires so much.

Drama queens tend towards pushing. As we discussed earlier, pushing is a very masculine outworking of energy. The feminine is all about flowing and swaying. Just *being*. There's a confidence without an arrogance that comes when we know who we are in our feminine. We cease having anything to prove because we are resolved. We stand in our truths with solidity. This is the power of our unshakeable inner she.

There is no judgement in my heart for the drama queens; they have been wounded. We can love such a sister into a new day of understanding. If she would just simply relax, own her crown, work with her inner she to understand fully who she is before the universe of love and light, we, her sisters, can help set her path straight.

The responsibility here is ours as women on a journey of the heart to help princesses become fully developed queens. Some of us will feel that call very deeply. Oh, it is much needed. Let's give the next generation of women everything we have within us so that in their time, they will be strong, magnificent, majestic queens.

*Killer Queens:* Now this type of woman is an evil queen. This is toxicity to the max. Sadly, killer queens cannot be helped or loved back into place by their sister queens. She wears a dark crown and delights in negativity, evil, trauma, and wounding. Maybe narcissism. Of course, they are severely wounded, and it is right to love them and feel compassion, but always safeguarding what is precious within us. This is the most important aspect. You see, if you are sitting on your throne in your queendom, you have ultimate permission about what goes on in your queendom. If it doesn't feel good to you, you do not have to have it. Period. Let that always be your yardstick. You are the queen, after all. If we allow these queens any space within our queendoms of pure light, they will attempt to usurp our thrones. They are soul killers. They can only come into a place of light through direct revelation to the universe themselves. One on one with the Universe. It upsets me to say it, as my heart wants to include everyone in my queendom, but we must not allow them a crown, a queendom, or a place in our queendoms. We must cut them loose for our sakes. For their sakes, it's sadly necessary.

Having the mindset of a queen is a very helpful analogy, I feel, in helping us really understand who we are in our feminine core, our inner she. In a real sense, it is more than an analogy. Before the universe we are crowned beings, crowned with our own glory. It's high time to own that, step into it, and claim for all its worth. I know that when we do that and become serious about our heart journey, everyone around us begins to notice and treats us differently. In accordance with our incredible queenship, let it be so.

# CHAPTER 11

# *A Gathered Sisterhood*

> This is the dawn of a new day, an ancient feminine wisdom, once hidden and silenced has awakened and is ready to Rise.
>
> —Rebecca Campbell, *Rise Sister Rise*

Darling sisters, I hope on this journey through this book together we've realised that we have so much power. More than we've ever realised. Certainly. In that realisation, we now need to magnify it tenfold, 100 million per cent. There is no limit.

We were never supposed to be lonely island girls stranded on a deserted island, writing SOS messages in the sand. I know that's exactly how we've been feeling. I've felt it for myself and know if I'm feeling that way, chances are you do too. It is a lonely place, being a 24/7 combination of wife/

mother/girlfriend/career girl in the workplace. Or single, living alone. When in our modern construct of society do we ever get to kick back and be girl in every facet? This girlness, our playful wildness, should not finish in us at age six. Our joys, our pleasures of being female should not be restricted to the abandon of our early childhood and only scratch the surface of wildness during adult consensual sexual encounters. Everything we can do to keep our wild hearts alive is important. We must try everything we can to ensure our young maidens receive a strong, correct message about the feminine from us. Not men, the media, advertising, or anyone who uses any method to influence our perception of femininity, exploiting our insecurities by focusing on them. The day has come when women need to receive and give life-affirming nourishment to the heart of each other. Announce it! With our sisters (and some brothers) who truly get it. The feminine within us validated. As our young girls put away their dolls or no longer skip through life and swap the wearing of pink in every item of clothing for navy, beige, or black, may their hearts be filled with the message and feeling that being a girl is all good. Of course, of course, my sisters, where are they going to get that message? Where does that seed get planted and rooted through the consistency of hearing it again and again? It can only be through us. We are the ones, the only ones, who can deliver that to the next generation.

What a sad travesty of the feminine when any of our hearts, at whatever age, come to believe, through whatever means, that our girlness is somehow and in some way wrong. For us, we need to reclaim the essence of the feminine. Preach it, sister!

Do we want more than a casual acquaintance with each other? We are not supposed to have a working relationship with our sisters but a heart connection. In terms of real depth

## Divine Purpose

and connection, we crave what our ancient sisters knew in their red tent way of life. Although we don't realise it, as it is unknown to us, our souls remember and long for it. We need it, and once we have it, we will understand that is like lifeblood to us.

In a gathered sisterhood, we have the power to change *everything*. As a combined force, we become "team girl". Imagine if every woman in the world had access to a small group of women who were equally committed to her welfare, her heart, her divine purpose as she is. Imagine how it could be if every young girl on starting her menstruation was endorsed as a woman in her own standing. Imagine if every single woman had the opportunity to be really heard, really seen, and really acknowledged. Imagine if every woman had the resources and the confidence through her sisters to fully explore and pursue her divine purpose. This is the power of our tribe. It truly is. It is all there for us in ways we are yet to even begin to consider possible. Such is the momentum of the ever-expanding universe that when we, together, intentionally plug into that life force, the love heart of the divine, everything will change. Together we can stand to bring to our world the end of oppression. That is what we have been given our superpowers for; that is what our divine purpose is all about. That is what stepping into our rightful places as a queen will achieve.

Sisters, this is the call. I can almost hear a sharp intake of breath as I write and you read these words. Both because our hearts sing with the recognition of something long forgotten and a little trepidation at stepping into a new day. Our vulnerabilities are on the line with each other as we open our hearts. This is exactly the place to be. We should not be in any fear of judgement from each other. Remember, there is no competition between queens. Never let us allow fear in any form to hold us back. We must find a way to gather, join our hearts, and rise in our power individually as a queen and together as a sisterhood.

Imagine a world without war, street violence, no patriarchy, no sexual or other types of abuse of any precious sister or child. My darlings, this is in our hands. We were never responsible for these horrible things, but if we come together, we can begin to make a huge impact on changing things for all time. This is our baton to pick up, run with, and pass on. It has to be us. Oppression can end if we find the strength in all of us not to tolerate any of these things on our doorsteps, in our own homes. We will be able to find a way because of our connectedness.

Imagine if we, all of us en masse did that. Each of us fulfilling our divine purpose, standing with each other. Helping each of us to stand in our truths, owning our queenships, owning our inner she, doing the heart work.

Can we get a glimpse of just how powerful we are? Here's the thing; there is no one else. My darling, there is only you and I and millions of our sisters. We have to face this. Males have run the show for a very long time, and patriarchy has given us many, many problems. The squashing and dumbing down of the precious feminine have not worked too well. For anyone. It is time, sisters. It is time. Do you hear the call?

It is time to end the greed, anger, hate, and the placing of profit making before the needs of humanity. The over-sexualisation of our children. The drug taking, the corruption, and the fear. If not us, then who?

Every beautiful sister needs and deserves the best opportunity to rise into her feminine. Her beautiful heart needs to shine and be seen. Let's find a way to become gathered, a powerful force.

## Divine Purpose

The answer is to connect, connect, connect, and then to go deep. The expansion of the feminine is never about going up levels, becoming more spiritual, more feminine than the next. No way; that's not how it is. In this place, where our feminine hearts are, our inner she is being made strong. We'll find in the most mysterious of ways that it is all about going down deep. Sometimes, though, to "get to the treasure we have to dig through mud." This is why it is essential that we help each other to get our hearts straight and deal with our past traumas, hurts, and experiences. Along with new difficulties that will come, and they will. It's all about how we walk forward in the light of our light. Do the heart work, look at our inner she, and make her strong. Feed our outer she good things. Walk in our divine purpose through our queendoms, and rise united as a oneness, a gathered sisterhood, where all of us are plugging into the universe of love and light and life. This is the path before us.

In very practical terms, there are a number of things we can do to enhance this.

- Gather your tribe. When we start to live intentionally in this way, we will find it draws like-minded souls to us. These precious sisters are our tribe. Research your local area; join a women's circle. If there isn't one, how about starting one? The red tent movement will help you get started with all that you need. Check out
https://redtentdirectory.com
www.redtenttemplemovement.com
Connect with a sister circle online. There are some great closed groups to ensure a modicum of privacy.

- Heart Maidens sister circle (which is our fabulous group)
- Rewilding for women
- Wild woman sisterhood
- Warrior Goddess tribe
  Or start your own.

  In our Heart Maidens Facebook group, members are also invited to participate in an online version of the red tent once a month through Messenger.

Come find us online at divinepurpose.co.uk.

- Develop a community of supportive women in your locality around a theme. It's okay to do this through a religious community or a local project that serves the specific needs of women in your area. Research and find out what is out there. Join it, start it, take it somewhere, and make it fly.
- Participate in trainings and retreats for women on a heart journey who wish to explore the divine feminine.

I hope you can see here that what we are saying is connect, connect, connect, connect, connect. In whatever context you feel led and called to. This is how we gather. I can hear the footsteps approaching. Girls, thank you for hearing my heart. This is awesome! As I write this, I feel as though I'm holding your hand, whispering in your ear, "We're on the move, we are on the move, and we are rising."

## CHAPTER 12

# *Rising and Flowing*

> A woman of substance, is able to make a life of substance.
>
> —Unknown

I've talked a lot—a lot—about rising. We all know what that means. It means to stand to our feet. For some of us, we've felt down and out spiritually speaking. We took a hammering through our wounds. We know the feminine has been severely wounded for us personally and as a sense of legacy in the messages Mother and others gave us about what "being female" means. Some of us are squashed and beaten down. We had the feminine essence trampled right out of our souls and find ourselves lying in the dirt, sobbing and eating crumbs, mourning the lost girl that we once or never were. Many of us have been wounded in our bodies because they are female, and we are survivors, overcomers, standing strong in truth and pain. Or we may be on a merry-go-round, a fairground ride that never ends, encompassing the two extremes of being too much and then again, not enough. Wherever we find ourselves, chances are this place is filled with many feelings of sadness. That is such a valid feeling. We are allowed to feel that, acknowledge it, and allow the universe into our hearts to turn that which came into our lives to detract value from us. We can take this pain and sadness and use it to build something strong, good, and sacred simply from our understanding. In a spiritual sense, knowing these things come from a place which has not been one of love our heart can begin turning toward light. Now, with our hearts aligned to a universe of love and light and life, we can come to the root of these feelings, and the fear can be dismantled. The concrete block of the pain can be smashed as we learn to build on love.

Darling, it's time to really face this head-on. I know that your spirit longs for more. Whilst my words in this book will do the job of an empowerer, as that is who I am in my divine purpose, the crazy truth is that I cannot empower a thing until our hearts step into agreement and alignment with the precious truths that the universe has for us. All I am able to speak are mere words.

Lining up with the universe of love and light and life, you'd be crazy to refuse that. So I know that your heart is with me. But it is your heart and free will that need the breath of empowerment to be revived. All I can do is be faithful to my calling before the universe and show you what it looks like. My heart and my spirit sing over you, that you would choose to join me. Not only join me, but take it from me, own it as your own, and fly with this for yourself. That is my heart for you.

My journey in writing this book has not been without cost. As I sit here writing tonight, I am recovering from

## Divine Purpose

severe back pain which has not allowed me to move my body properly for a number of days. Here I sit, asking us to stand to our feet and rise. I have cried many tears of pain (physical and emotional) as the universe has seemingly rooted me for this season to bring what I feel is liquid gold from my heart. I cannot be anything other than grateful for this honour and privilege.

When we rise, we do so from the heart first. The body and our actions are just following through to confirm to our hearts that we mean it. We mean business; we commit to it. In other words, we put our money where our mouths are.

Rising is all about taking that beaten-down, squashed sense of the feminine deep inside us and breathing life into her once again. This is where the work of the inner she is so important. We are taking our smallness and making it big using the process we've shared together. It is important to understand what we mean when we talk about rising. The opposite of it is deadly. We remain unfulfilled, weak, and defeated. By default, the woman who is not risen is lying on the floor. That pure heart becomes a doormat for others to walk on, or an insignificant crumb to be swept away. Do you see how important this is? Queen, that is not your place or space to occupy. Rise, my dearest one.

Being in flow is all about lining up our hearts to be in tune with the universe. The feminine is all about flow. There is nothing about us, not one thing, that is like a straight edge. Just look at your body. The curvier the better! We weave, we flow, we blend, we intertwine. There is, in fact, no end to our feminine essence. We know how to mingle with our sisters to become collaborators for our mutual benefits. It is a mystery of the "woman nature" that we know how to do this instinctively. We certainly know how to intertwine with the masculine on a sexual basis. Here we connect the deep to the deep of both of these energies. Even if a child is not created from that union, something unseen in our physical realm is. There is an explosion of energy when life is released through the climax of sexual union. Women feel it so strongly that it often moves us to tears after an orgasm. It is an incredible life force.

We can enhance the flow of love and life energy simply by welcoming and embracing it. It's all about connection. As a reminder, we talked about connecting with the universe through the natural world. When we are mindful and intentional about this, we are unblocked. We flow free as a river. Have you ever seen a wild river that didn't flow and bend and curve through the land following its easiest path? I have never seen a straight river in my life. The feminine is exactly like that. Jump in, sister. Get wet all over with this river for she is wonderful!

Flow produces a clear mindset. We become very sure about the path before us. Not because we are making a logical plan, but because of our trust in the universe and in our divine purpose, our fulfilment of it, knowing so deeply we have been uniquely chosen. It gives us all the self-assuredness that we need. Of course, because we have aligned our hearts to the universe, we have made space for the universe to teach us about our hearts and to guide us in our footsteps as we encompass our divine purposes. We are finally open, able to hear all things about ourselves to ensure that we keep on walking in alignment with the universe of love and light. Talk about holding space. This is the ultimate in the universe holding space for us within itself. Once we know it in the deep core of the feminine, we will never want to be out of the flow of that river again.

Yes, it is all about connection, connection, connection; it does come first. Or we could say alignment, lining up

## Divine Purpose

with the universe. That is because the conscious part of us makes the intentional commitment to move to a place where we can be open enough to receive from source, our inner she, and from each other. That is true flow coming straight out of that place. We are ready to take a step into our divine purpose.

So divinely beautiful. It is indeed "liquid gold".

## CHAPTER 13

# *Legacy of a Heart Maiden*

> Her children rise up and call her blessed:
> Many women have done excellently,
> but you surpass them all.
> —Proverbs 31:28–29, King Lemuel's mother

The universe gave me the sense of naming our sister circle Facebook group *Heart Maidens* in the middle of 2017. It is an extraordinary term. That came right out my spirit to express my desire to connect with women who are on similar journeys of the heart as I am. Inside me is this longing to connect.

My joy bubbles over whenever we add a new sister to our group and we meet in our own red tent through Messenger. It is exquisitely profound.

Then I felt led by the universe to become even more

## Divine Purpose

directional in bringing clarity in describing what divine purpose is and bringing it in for us all.

Morgan and I developed our divine purpose Facebook group so that we are able to share our thoughts and feelings on what divine purpose means to us personally. It is a very safe place for us to come and ask our questions and get support as we journey together. We truly would love to see you join us there and meet you as we share our beautiful hearts together. It is a magnificent journey. It's exciting and beautiful and awesome all at the same time. The universe strongly led me to write this book. I felt a birthing in my spirit in order to get my heart out there into yours. So I release my words. I gift them to you and to the universe, who sent me to share them through the work of my own divine purpose.

The way to understand flow, in all its gorgeousness, is to notice that we are in a golden thread of women. There is no break in the chain. Women give birth to girls who then become women. We are the daughters of those precious ancient sisters in their original red tents. They are our heritage, and we are their legacy as we will become the heritage for the daughters of the earth whom we raise. And they are our legacies. We owe them this gift. It is a precious pearl, a pearl that they can pass down through the generations to create their own legacies. We remember all those beautiful women who have gone before us, and often at a very dear cost to themselves, sometimes paid for with their lives. For the ones beaten and tortured, burnt at the stake, beheaded, murdered, persecuted, raped, abused so that they could buy a better day for our freedom from oppression, we honour their sacrifice. What better way to honour these dear ones who bravely went before us than to continue passing on that same pure legacy to rise for all the daughters of the earth in the fullness of our own divine purpose. So that our legacy holders, our daughters, the beautiful maidens of the future may know without any fear, restriction, or rejection that to stand in the truth of their feminine is the proper order of things. The truth of who they are, loved and held by the depths of the earth and the universe that sent them.

Within ourselves, our flow between us and our life force, the universe gets switched on when our feminine essence awakens. Cultivating it through understanding of our inner she, our outer she, and how we are designed to hold our queenships creates flow. It's all a beautiful, golden weave. As we become intentional, mindful about our place in right standing before the universe, the feminine essence explodes in us. We have become open through our intentionality to receive. So, dear sister, we shall. In that wonderful, gorgeous, held space, we find our divine purpose.

It is time, high time, beyond time. Let's change this world. Let's rise and stand as one in our divine purpose so that the world may know the power, majesty, and grace of a woman in all her glory. And let that woman be you.

References and Further Reading

- Rebecca Campbell, *Rise Sister Rise*. Hay House UK.
- Molesey Crawford, *Unlocking the Queen Code*. Legacy of Timbuktu.
- Paul Scanlon, *Events versus Process*. Abundant Life Publishing.
- Rachel Jayne Groover, *Powerful and Feminine*. Rachel Jayne Groover.
- Sharon Blackie, *If Women Rose Rooted*. September Publishing.

**Divine Purpose**

- Clarissa Pinkola Estes, *Women Who Run with the Wolves*. Rider.
- Judyth Vary Baker, *Me and Lee*. Trine Day.
- Anita Diarmant, *The Red Tent*. Pan.
- *Heather Ash Amara, Warrior Goddess Training*. Hay House UK.
- Don Miguel Ruiz, *The Four Agreements*. Amber-Allen Publishing.
- *Revised authorised, Holy Bible*. www.biblegateway.com.

CPSIA information can be obtained
at www.ICGtesting.com
Printed in the USA
BVHW081107200819
556319BV00013B/1193/P